THE KIT

PIZZAS &
PASTA

THE KITCHEN LIBRARY
PIZZAS & PASTA

Caroline Ellwood

HAMLYN

CONTENTS

This edition published in 1990 by
The Hamlyn Publishing Group Limited,
a division of the Octopus Publishing Group,
Michelin House, 81 Fulham Road,
London SW3 6RB

© Cathay Books 1985

ISBN 0 600 56938 1

Produced by Mandarin Offset
Printed and Bound in Hong Kong

INTRODUCTION

Pizzas and pasta are becoming increasingly popular. Having enjoyed them on holiday or in restaurants everyone now wants to try cooking them.

This cookbook offers you easy-to-follow recipes with an authentic Italian flavour. I have collected many of them during visits to Italy and from Italian friends. They are all easy to prepare. Whether you try making the basic doughs or buy ready-made ones, you can add your favourite ingredients to sauces to give an individual flavour.

The important thing to remember with the preparation of any food – but especially Italian – is that the ingredients should be as fresh as possible. For instance, the use of fresh Parmesan cheese is essential to the flavour of the recipes; the pre-packed variety will not do, as it adds a strong, pungent taste which ruins the overall flavour of the dish.

Fresh herbs are also important. It is worth growing your own marjoram, oregano and basil in a kitchen windowbox as they add a special flavour to sauces which is far superior to that of their dried equivalents. It is also preferable to use freshly made stock rather than stock cubes.

These recipes will remind you of happy times spent in Italy, or tempt you to visit this beautiful country. Enjoy cooking, serving and eating them.

NOTES

Standard spoon measurements are used in all recipes
1 tablespoon = one 15 ml spoon
1 teaspoon = one 5 ml spoon
All spoon measures are level.

Fresh herbs are used unless otherwise stated. If unobtainable substitute a bouquet garni of the equivalent dried herbs, or use dried herbs instead but halve the quantities stated.

Use freshly ground black pepper where pepper is specified.

If fresh yeast is unobtainable, substitute dried yeast but use only half the stated quantity and follow the manufacturer's instructions for reconstituting.

Ovens should be preheated to the specified temperature.

For all recipes, quantities are given in both metric and imperial measures. Follow either set but not a mixture of both, because they are not interchangeable.

Recipes for basic pasta and pizza doughs are given in the introductory copy. Detailed instructions for cooking pasta are given in the introduction. Refer to these where the copy is marked with an asterisk.

PASTA

Pasta is one of the easiest dishes in the world to prepare. It is also one of the easiest to ruin. More often than not, it is ruined by not following a few essential cooking rules.

Pasta is a good source of protein and the wholewheat variety has a high fibre content. If you are counting calories, reduce the amount of butter and oil used in the recipes and choose a sauce which is low in calories.

As well as the many dried varieties of pasta available, an increasing number of stores now sell fresh pasta. This is, by far, preferable to the dried type as it is very near the flavour and texture of homemade pasta.

Anyone who is adept at pastry-making will have no trouble in making their own pasta. It may take a few practice runs, but it is well worth the trouble. Don't give up after the first attempt – practice really does make perfect. Homemade pasta has an individual flavour which will certainly be appreciated.

Most of the recipes in this book use fresh pasta, which can be the bought variety or your own homemade if time allows. Allow about 125 g (4 oz) fresh pasta per person for a main course, depending on how substantial the sauce is and the size of the appetite, and about 50 g (2 oz) for a starter. If dried pasta is used, it is specified in the recipe. If you choose to use a dried variety instead of fresh, allow 50-75 g (2-3 oz) dried pasta per person for a main course, and 25-50 g (1-2 oz) for a starter.

The pasta dough on page 10 can be used to make all types of pasta. It is referred to in the recipes as '500 g (1 lb) quantity pasta dough', where it is intended homemade dough should be used, although you may buy it ready-made in the piece if preferred. If you use the dough recipe to make your own tagliatelle, etc, either adjust the basic recipe to give you the amount specified, or make it all up and keep any leftover pasta dough in the freezer for up to 3 months.

Cooking Pasta

All pasta must be cooked in plenty of water. As a guide, allow at least 4 litres (7 pints) water for 500 g (1 lb) pasta. Never use less than 3 litres (5¼ pints) even for a small amount. Do not attempt to cook more than 1 kg (2 lb) in one pan, as it is difficult to stir, season and drain. The addition of oil prevents the pasta pieces from sticking together.

Bring the water, 1-2 tablespoons oil and 1-2 tablespoons salt to the boil. Add the pasta, return to the boil and ensure that the pasta is well covered with water.

Cook uncovered, stirring occasionally, until *al dente* – just tender but firm to the bite. For fresh pasta this will take about 2 to 3 minutes (10 to 15 minutes for filled types); dried pasta will take about 9 to 12 minutes. Do *not* simply follow the

manufacturer's cooking times or the recipe – test the pasta frequently during cooking. Pasta that is overcooked and soft is unappetizing.

As soon as it is *al dente*, drain the pasta to stop it softening further, toss in butter and coat in sauce to prevent it drying out. Serve immediately, accompanied by freshly grated Parmesan.

Types of Pasta

The varieties of pasta are endless. Freshly made tagliatelle, fettuccine and spaghetti are available in good supermarkets and delicatessens, as well as some stuffed varieties such as tortellini and ravioli.

There is an excellent range of dried pasta in most stores. A selection of the many varieties available is illustrated overleaf. For those of us in a hurry, there is an excellent dried lasagne on the market which requires no pre-cooking, so it can be used in the same way as freshly made lasagne. Follow the manufacturer's instructions for its use.

DRIED PASTA VARIETIES

1. Pasta twists
2. Tortellini
3. Pasta bow ties
4. Pasta shells
5. Wholewheat macaroni
6. Pasta whirls
7. Pasta spirals
8. Tagliatelle verdi
9. Tagliatelle
10. Wholewheat tagliatelle

11. Rigatoni
12. Small pasta shells
13. Wholewheat spaghetti
14. Pasta wheels
15. Spaghetti

16. Vermicelli
17. Lasagne verdi
18. Lasagne
19. Wholewheat rigatoni
20. Pasta quills

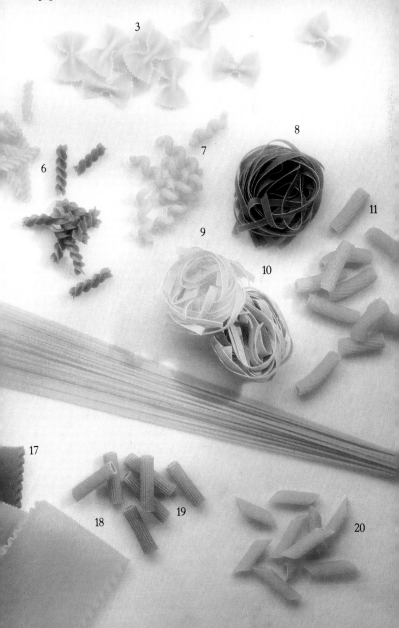

EGG PASTA DOUGH

500 g (1 lb) plain flour
good pinch of salt
2 large or 3 medium eggs
1 teaspoon oil
3-4 tablespoons water

Sift the flour and salt into a large bowl. Make a hollow in the centre and drop in the eggs and oil. Draw the flour into the centre, add 3 tablespoons water and knead well; add another tablespoon of water if the mixture is too dry.

Knead the dough until smooth and very elastic; this is essential, or the dough will not roll properly. Wrap the dough in clingfilm and leave to rest for a minimum of 15 minutes and a maximum of 2 hours.

Makes a 500 g (1 lb) quantity
NOTE: For wholemeal pasta, use 500 g (1 lb) wholemeal flour, 3 large eggs and about 4-5 tablespoons water.

SPINACH AND EGG PASTA DOUGH

350 g (12 oz) plain flour
good pinch of salt
125 g (4 oz) cooked leaf
spinach, well drained
and finely chopped
2 large or 3 medium eggs
1 teaspoon oil

Follow the directions for the basic egg pasta dough (above), adding the spinach with the eggs.

Makes a 500 g (1 lb) quantity
NOTE: This pasta is easier to make than the egg pasta. It is easier to work as it does not dry out as quickly.

To Roll Out Pasta Dough

Roll out the dough on a lightly floured board or in a pasta machine. Rolling by hand is preferable, but a pasta machine makes the job a lot easier and quicker. If using a machine, follow the manufacturer's instructions.

The rolling process is very important and it is well worth taking the time to achieve a good result. Do not give up if the first result is inedible and disappointing – practice certainly does make perfect in this instance.

Flatten the dough with the rolling pin, giving the dough a quarter turn between each roll, until it measures 20-23 cm (8-9 inches) in diameter.

Hold the near edge of the dough down with one hand and place the rolling pin on the opposite edge. Push the rolling pin as follows to stretch the dough; *do not roll*. Curl the end of the dough around the pin and push with the pin to stretch the dough. Keep moving the pin towards you along the dough, stopping, stretching the dough, then rolling up more dough, until you have taken up all the dough. Give the pin a quarter turn so that it points towards you and unfurl the sheet of dough, opening it up flat.

Repeat the rolling and stretching until the dough is once again completely wrapped around the pin. Turn the pin round again, unwrap the dough and repeat the procedure. Continue until a 500 g (1 lb) quantity pasta dough has been stretched to a square measuring about 40-45 cm (16-18 inches). This process must be done very quickly to prevent the dough drying out; if this happens, it will be ruined.

Roll out the dough until it is paper thin, then use as required.

PIZZAS

There are three ways of making basic pizza doughs. The one I recommend is the traditional bread dough, which is made with strong flour and yeast. This is the one specified for all the recipes in this book.

If time is short, a packet of commercially made bread mix can be used instead. It is equally good and has the advantage of being quick and very easy. Follow the packet instructions exactly, then roll out evenly and use as indicated in each recipe.

Ready-made pizza bases and jars of pizza sauce are available from many supermarkets – a definite boon when you need an instant snack.

As a last resort, a scone dough can be used – but please don't expect the same results. It is a very poor substitute and does not give a real Italian texture or flavour.

PIZZA DOUGH

200 g (7 oz) plain flour
1 teaspoon salt
1 tablespoon olive oil
15 g (½ oz) fresh yeast,
* or 1 packet easy blend*
* dried yeast*

Sift the flour and salt into a large bowl. Add the oil and yeast and knead to a soft, elastic dough; this will take about 8 minutes by hand or 4 to 5 minutes in a food processor or electric blender. Cover and leave to rise in a warm place for 2½ to 3 hours, until doubled in size.

Makes one 25 cm (10 inch) pizza

To Roll Out Pizza Dough

Place the dough on a floured board and knead lightly. Roll out to a 25-30 cm (10-12 inch) circle, about 5 mm (¼ inch) thick, turning the dough as it is rolled to prevent shrinking. Using the fingertips, push some of the dough from the centre towards the edge, making the edge about twice as thick as the rest of the circle.

Place the dough on a lightly floured piece of circular cardboard and proceed as directed in each recipe. Assembling the pizza on a cardboard circle makes it easier to transfer to the baking sheet.

If the recipe states 'place the pizza on a hot baking sheet', put the baking sheet in the oven to warm while preheating the oven. Leave it in there until it is really hot. This is most important, as it ensures that the pizza will have a crisp base and that the top and base will cook evenly.

PASTA STARTERS

TAGLIATELLE WITH ASPARAGUS

75 g (3 oz) butter
2 cloves garlic, crushed
500 g (1 lb) thin asparagus spears, cut into 2.5 cm (1 inch) lengths
284 ml (½ pint) double cream
1 tablespoon each chopped parsley and thyme
salt and pepper
500 g (1 lb) fresh tagliatelle
50 g (2 oz) Parmesan cheese, grated
thyme or parsley sprigs to garnish

Heat 50 g (2 oz) of the butter in a wok or frying pan, add the garlic and asparagus and cook gently, without browning, for 7 to 10 minutes, until the asparagus is just tender. Add the cream, herbs, and salt and pepper to taste. Remove from the heat.

Cook the pasta until *al dente**. Drain thoroughly and turn into a warmed serving dish. Add the remaining butter and toss well.

Return the sauce to the heat for 1 minute, then pour over the pasta. Sprinkle with the Parmesan cheese and garnish with thyme or parsley sprigs. Serve immediately.

Serves 6

FETTUCCINE WITH COURGETTES

*750 g (1½ lb) young
  courgettes*
salt
50 g (2 oz) plain flour
oil for shallow frying
4 cloves garlic
*500 g (1 lb) fresh
  fettuccine or fine
  noodles*
50 g (2 oz) butter
*12 basil leaves, torn into 2
  or 3 pieces*
*50 g (2 oz) Parmesan
  cheese, grated*
basil sprigs to garnish

Cut the courgettes into 5 cm (2 inch) lengths and arrange in layers in a colander, sprinkling each layer liberally with salt. Leave to drain for 1 to 2 hours. Rinse well and dry thoroughly on kitchen paper. Toss in the flour.

Heat the oil in a frying pan, add the whole garlic cloves and fry until coloured, then remove. Add the courgettes in batches and fry until golden. Drain on kitchen paper and keep hot.

Meanwhile, cook the pasta until *al dente**. Drain and turn into a warmed serving dish. Add the butter and basil and toss well. Stir in the courgettes, sprinkle with the cheese and garnish with basil. Serve immediately.

Serves 6

MEAT-STUFFED CANNELLONI

1 tablespoon oil
1 large onion, chopped
1 clove garlic, crushed
175 g (6 oz) minced beef
50 g (2 oz) Mortadella,
  chopped
½ teaspoon dried mixed
  herbs
pinch of grated nutmeg
salt and pepper
1 egg yolk
250 g (8 oz) Ricotta or
  curd cheese
125 g (4 oz) Parmesan
  cheese, grated
250 g (8 oz) quantity
  pasta dough*

MEAT SAUCE:
1 tablespoon oil
1 onion, chopped
1 clove garlic, crushed
175 g (6 oz) minced beef
6 tomatoes
1 tablespoon each chopped
  basil and marjoram
150 ml (¼ pint) dry
  white wine

TOPPING:
175 g (6 oz) Mozzarella
  cheese, sliced
2 tablespoons grated
  Parmesan cheese
2 tablespoons dried
  breadcrumbs

Heat the oil in a pan, add the onion and garlic and cook for 2 minutes, without browning. Increase the heat, add the beef and brown quickly.

Add the Mortadella, herbs, nutmeg, and salt and pepper to taste. Cook, uncovered, for 15 minutes, stirring occasionally. Remove from the heat, stir in the egg yolk and cheeses and mix well. Set aside to cool.

To make the meat sauce, heat the oil in a pan, add the onion and garlic and cook for 2 minutes, without browning. Increase the heat, add the beef and brown quickly.

Skin, seed and chop the tomatoes, and add to the pan with the herbs, and salt and pepper to taste. Pour over the wine, bring to the boil and cook rapidly for 15 to 20 minutes, until reduced and thickened. Set aside.

Cut the pasta dough into 7.5 × 10 cm (3 × 4 inch) sheets and cook until just *al dente**. Drain thoroughly and lay on clean dry tea–towels.

Divide the stuffing between the pasta sheets and roll up from the shorter side. Arrange in a single layer, seam side down, in a lightly greased ovenproof dish. Spoon over the sauce.

Place the Mozzarella cheese slices on top and sprinkle with the Parmesan and breadcrumbs. Bake in a preheated moderately hot oven, 200°C (400°F), Gas Mark 6, for 15 to 20 minutes, until golden brown. Serve immediately.

Serves 6 to 8

NOTE: This may also be served as a main course for 4 people.

SPAGHETTI WITH TOMATO AND CHEESE SAUCE

1 kg (2 lb) tomatoes
1 celery stick
1 carrot, chopped
2 onions, chopped
150 ml (¼ pint) dry
   white wine
2 tablespoons chopped
   marjoram
25 g (1 oz) matured
   Cheddar cheese, grated
2 tablespoons grated
   Parmesan cheese
salt and pepper
500 g (1 lb) fresh
   spaghetti
25 g (1 oz) butter

Roughly chop the tomatoes and celery and place in a pan with the carrot and onions. Bring slowly to the boil, cover and simmer for 30 minutes. Rub through a sieve and return to the pan.

Add the wine, bring to the boil and cook for 15 to 20 minutes, until the sauce has reduced and thickened. Remove from the heat and stir in the marjoram, cheeses, and salt and pepper to taste.

Cook the spaghetti until *al dente**. Drain thoroughly and turn into a warmed serving dish. Add the butter and toss well. Heat the sauce thoroughly and pour over the pasta. Serve immediately.
Serves 6

NOODLES WITH SWEET PEPPER SAUCE

2 red peppers
250 g (8 oz) tomatoes
2 tablespoons oil
1 onion, chopped
salt and pepper
250 g (8 oz) Italian
  salami, chopped
250 g (8 oz) fresh egg
  tagliatelle
250 g (8 oz) fresh
  tagliatelle verdi
25 g (1 oz) butter
25 g (1 oz) Parmesan
  cheese, grated
  (optional)
TO GARNISH:
red pepper slices
thyme sprigs

Remove the core and seeds from the peppers. Peel thinly and cut into 1 cm (½ inch) squares. Skin, seed and chop the tomatoes.

Heat the oil in a pan, add the onion and cook for 5 minutes, until golden brown, stirring. Lower heat, add the peppers and cook for 7 to 8 minutes, until soft, stirring occasionally.

Add the tomatoes and cook for 3 minutes. Season liberally with salt and pepper. Add the salami, check the seasoning and remove from the heat.

Meanwhile, cook the pasta until *al dente**. Drain thoroughly and turn into a warmed serving dish. Add the butter and toss well.

Return the sauce to the heat and boil for 1 minute. Pour over the pasta, sprinkle with the Parmesan cheese, if using, and garnish with pepper slices and thyme. Serve immediately.
Serves 6

CRESCIONI

500 g (1 lb) quantity
  pasta dough*
750 g (1½ lb) spinach
25 g (1 oz) butter
1-2 cloves garlic, crushed
80 g (3 oz) Boursin
  cheese with garlic
pinch of grated nutmeg
1 tablespoon each chopped
  chives, parsley and
  marjoram
salt and pepper
a little beaten egg
oil for shallow frying
3-4 tablespoons grated
  Parmesan cheese

Roll out the pasta dough very thinly, cover with clingfilm and leave to rest for 5 minutes.

Cook the spinach, with just the water clinging to the leaves after washing, for 3 minutes. Drain well and chop roughly.

Melt the butter in a frying pan, add the garlic and cook for 2 minutes, without browning. Stir in the spinach, cheese, nutmeg, herbs, salt to taste and lots of pepper.

Cut the pasta into 7.5 cm (3 inch) squares. Place a teaspoon of the filling in the centre of each square, brush the edges with beaten egg, fold over like a turnover and seal firmly. Place on a tea-towel to dry for 1 hour. Heat the oil in a frying pan, add a few crescioni at a time and fry for 3 minutes each side, until golden. Drain on kitchen paper and place in a warmed dish.

Sprinkle with the Parmesan cheese and serve immediately.
Serves 6

TAGLIATELLE WITH FOUR CHEESES

50 g (2 oz) butter
1 onion, chopped
2-3 cloves garlic, crushed
125 g (4 oz) streaky
    bacon, derinded and
    diced
75 g (3 oz) each Bel
    Paese, matured
    Cheddar and Gruyère
    cheese, grated
50 g (2 oz) Parmesan
    cheese, grated
284 ml (½ pint) double
    cream
500 g (1 lb) fresh
    wholewheat tagliatelle
2 tablespoons each
    chopped parsley and
    chives
1 tablespoon chopped basil

Melt half the butter in a saucepan, add the onion and garlic and cook, without browning, for 2 to 3 minutes. Add the bacon and cook for 5 minutes, stirring occasionally. Stir in the cheeses and cream. Remove from the heat.

Cook the pasta until *al dente**. Drain thoroughly and turn into a warmed serving dish. Add the remaining butter and toss well.

Return the sauce to the heat and stir in the herbs. Pour over the pasta and mix well. Serve immediately.
Serves 4 to 6

SPAGHETTI WITH GARLIC AND OIL

500 g (1 lb) fresh
  spaghetti
10 tablespoons olive oil
4 cloves garlic, crushed
25 g (1 oz) butter
3 tablespoons chopped
  parsley

Cook the spaghetti until *al dente**.

Meanwhile, heat the oil in a pan, add the garlic and fry until golden, stirring constantly.

Drain the spaghetti and turn into a warmed serving dish. Add the butter and toss well. Pour over the oil and garlic and mix well. Stir in the parsley and serve immediately.

Serves 6

RAVIOLI ALLA FIORENTINA

1 kg (2 lb) spinach
125 g (4 oz) butter
25 g (1 oz) plain flour
250 g (8 oz) Ricotta or
  curd cheese
3 egg yolks
pinch of grated nutmeg
salt and pepper
50 g (2 oz) Parmesan
  cheese, grated
lime or lemon slices to
  garnish (optional)

Cook the spinach, with just the water clinging to its leaves after washing, for 3 minutes. Drain and cool under cold running water. Drain thoroughly and press well with the hands to remove all the moisture. Chop finely and set aside.

Melt 25 g (1 oz) of the butter in a pan, stir in the flour and cook for 2 minutes, stirring. Add the Ricotta or curd cheese.

Lower the heat and add the spinach, egg yolks, nutmeg, and salt and pepper to taste. Cook, stirring constantly, for 1 minute, taking care not to curdle the egg. Remove from the heat and leave until completely cold.

Roll into pointed sausage shapes about 2.5 cm (1 inch) in length and place on a board to dry for 1 hour.

Cook in batches, in boiling salted water, for about 4 minutes; they are cooked when they rise to the surface. Remove with a slotted spoon and place in a warmed serving dish.

Add the remaining butter and toss well. Sprinkle with the Parmesan. Garnish with lime or lemon slices if liked, and serve immediately.

Serves 6

NOODLES WITH FISH SAUCE

10 anchovies
2-3 tablespoons milk
75 g (3 oz) butter
1 large onion, chopped
1-2 cloves garlic, very
   thinly sliced
150 ml (¼ pint) dry
   white wine
250 ml (8 fl oz) fish stock
   (see below)
175 g (6 oz) peeled
   prawns
salt and pepper
2-3 tablespoons chopped
   parsley
500 g (1 lb) fresh noodles
TO GARNISH:
anchovy fillets
whole prawns

Soak the anchovies in the milk for
30 minutes, drain, chop and set aside.

Melt 50 g (2 oz) of the butter in a
pan, add the onion and cook until
golden brown. Add the garlic and
cook for 1 minute. Add the wine,
bring to the boil and cook rapidly
until reduced by half. Add the fish
stock, anchovies, prawns, and salt
and pepper to taste and cook,
uncovered, for 2 minutes. Remove
from the heat and stir in the parsley.

Cook the noodles until al dente*.
Drain thoroughly and turn into a
warmed serving dish. Add the
remaining butter and toss well.

Heat the sauce for 1 minute, pour
over the noodles and toss well.
Garnish with a lattice of anchovy
fillets and whole prawns. Serve
immediately with Parmesan cheese.

Serves 6

NOTE: To make fish stock, place fish
heads and bones in a large pan with
1 onion, 1 carrot and a bouquet garni.
Cover with cold water, bring to the
boil, then simmer for 1 hour; strain.

RAVIOLI WITH CHICKEN

125 g (4 oz) butter
1 small onion, chopped
50 g (2 oz) button
  mushrooms, diced
750 g (1½ lb) cooked
  chicken, minced
120 ml (4 fl oz) dry white
  wine
120 ml (4 fl oz) single
  cream
1 tablespoon chopped
  parsley
salt and pepper
500 g (1 lb) quantity
  pasta dough*
1 beaten egg
4-6 tablespoons grated
  Parmesan cheese
parsley sprigs to garnish

Melt 25 g (1 oz) of the butter in a pan, add the onion and cook for 5 minutes, without browning. Add mushrooms and cook for 2 minutes. Remove from the heat and stir in the chicken, wine, cream, parsley, and salt and pepper to taste. Leave until cold.

Cut the pasta in half. Cover with clingfilm and rest for 30 minutes.

Place teaspoons of the chicken mixture about 5 cm (2 inches) apart on one piece of pasta. Brush lightly with beaten egg between the filling.

Lay the second sheet of pasta lightly on top, pressing down between the filling to seal. Cut around the filling with a pastry wheel or knife to give little ravioli squares. Check that each ravioli is thoroughly sealed and place on a board to dry for 1 hour.

Cook until *al dente**. Transfer to a warmed serving dish with a slotted spoon. Add the remaining butter and toss well. Sprinkle with Parmesan cheese to taste and garnish with parsley. Serve immediately.

Serves 6

SEAFOOD CANNELLONI

2 celery sticks, chopped
2 carrots, chopped
600 ml (1 pint) milk
1 onion, quartered
3 peppercorns
1 bay leaf
50 g (2 oz) butter
50 g (2 oz) plain flour
1 tablespoon chopped dill
2 tablespoons chopped
    parsley
salt and pepper
250 g (8 oz) quantity
    pasta dough*
1 tablespoon oil
2 tablespoons dried
    breadcrumbs
FILLING:
150 ml (¼ pint) dry
    white wine
4 scallops, shelled and
    halved
15 g (½ oz) butter
2 spring onions, chopped
250 g (8 oz) peeled
    prawns
125 g (4 oz) matured
    Cheddar cheese, grated
4 tablespoons grated
    Parmesan cheese
TO GARNISH:
whole prawns
dill sprigs

Put the celery and carrots in a pan with the milk, onion, peppercorns and bay leaf. Bring to the boil, remove from the heat and leave until cold. Strain and set aside the milk.

Melt the butter in a pan, stir in the flour and cook for 2 minutes, stirring. Gradually add the milk, stirring constantly. Bring to the boil and cook for 2 minutes, stirring. Stir in the herbs and salt to taste.

To make the filling, place the wine in a small pan and bring to the boil. Add the scallops and cook, uncovered, for about 2 minutes, until tender. Remove with a slotted spoon and set aside. Reserve the wine.

Melt the butter in a pan, add the spring onions and cook, without browning, for 1 minute. Add the reserved wine and boil for 1 to 2 minutes until reduced to about 2 tablespoons. Remove from the heat, stir in just over a quarter of the sauce and mix well. Add the prawns, scallops, and salt and pepper to taste. Stir in the cheeses, heating if necessary to melt.

Cut the pasta dough into 7.5 × 10 cm (3 × 4 inch) sheets and cook in boiling salted water, with the oil added, for 1 minute. Drain thoroughly and lay on clean dry tea-towels.

Divide the filling between the pasta sheets and roll up from the shorter side. Arrange in a single layer, seam side down, in a lightly greased ovenproof dish. Spoon over the sauce and sprinkle with the breadcrumbs.

Cook in a preheated moderately hot oven, 200°C (400°F), Gas Mark 6, for 15 to 20 minutes, until golden. Garnish with prawns and dill and serve immediately.

Serves 6 to 8
NOTE: This may also be served as a main course for 4 people.

NOODLES WITH PISTOU

4 cloves garlic
about 35 basil leaves
about 25 marjoram leaves
50 g (2 oz) butter
284 ml (½ pint) double
    cream
salt and pepper
500 g (1 lb) fresh noodles
150 g (5 oz) Parmesan
    cheese, grated
basil or marjoram sprigs to
    garnish

Crush the garlic and finely chop the herbs. Mix together well. Melt half the butter in a pan, remove from the heat, stir in the cream, and season well with salt and pepper.

Cook the noodles until *al dente**. Drain well and turn into a warmed serving dish. Add the remaining butter and toss well.

Return the sauce to the heat and stir in the cheese until melted. Pour over the noodles and toss well. Garnish with basil or marjoram and serve immediately.

Serves 6

PIZZAS

SMOKED SALMON AND DILL PIZZA

1 quantity pizza dough*
3 Marmande or Provence
  tomatoes, skinned and
  sliced
175 g (6 oz) smoked
  salmon, thinly sliced
1 tablespoon each chopped
  dill and parsley
125 g (4 oz) Mozzarella
  cheese, sliced

Roll out the dough*. Arrange the tomatoes on the base and lay the salmon on top. Sprinkle with the herbs and cover with the cheese.

Slide the pizza onto a hot baking sheet* and bake at once in a preheated hot oven, 220°C (425°F), Gas Mark 7, for 15 to 20 minutes, until golden. Serve immediately.

Serves 4

NOTE: For a less expensive variation, use peeled prawns instead of salmon.

ROMAN PIZZA

1 quantity pizza dough*
4 Marmande or Provence
  tomatoes, skinned and
  sliced
6 basil leaves, finely
  chopped
1 tablespoon chopped
  oregano
salt and pepper
125 g (4 oz) Parma ham,
  thinly sliced
50 g (2 oz) button
  mushrooms
75 g (3 oz) matured
  Cheddar cheese, grated

Roll out the dough*. Arrange the
tomatoes on the base, sprinkle with
the herbs, and season with salt and
pepper to taste. Lay the Parma ham
on top and sprinkle with the
mushrooms and cheese.
   Slide the pizza onto a hot baking
sheet* and bake at once in a preheated
hot oven, 220°C (425°F), Gas Mark 7,
until golden. Serve immediately.
Serves 4

TOMATO AND MOZZARELLA PIZZA

500 g (1 lb) ripe plum
  tomatoes, or 1 × 397 g
  (14 oz) can tomatoes
2 tablespoons olive oil
1 teaspoon salt
1 quantity pizza dough*
175 g (6 oz) Mozzarella
  cheese, grated
1 teaspoon dried oregano
1 tablespoon grated
  Parmesan cheese

Roughly chop the tomatoes and
place, with their juice, in a frying
pan. Add the oil and salt, bring to the
boil, cover and cook for 2 minutes.
Remove the lid and simmer for
15 minutes, stirring occasionally,
until thickened.

Turn the mixture into a sieve and
discard any liquid that drains
through. Rub the tomatoes through
the sieve and leave to cool.

Roll out the dough*. Sprinkle with
the Mozzarella cheese, spoon over the
tomato sauce, then sprinkle with the
oregano and Parmesan.

Slide the pizza onto a hot baking
sheet* and bake in a preheated hot
oven, 230°C (450°F), Gas Mark 8, for
15 to 20 minutes, until golden brown.
Serve immediately.
Serves 4

PIZZA PAYSANNE

50 g (2 oz) butter
1 large onion, finely
  chopped
4 rashers streaky bacon,
  derinded and chopped
2 potatoes, diced
2 eggs
142 ml (5 fl oz) double
  cream
1 tablespoon each chopped
  parsley, thyme and
  chives
salt and pepper
1 quantity pizza dough*
1 small red pepper, cored,
  seeded and chopped
125 g (4 oz) matured
  Cheddar cheese, grated

Melt the butter in a pan, add the
onion and bacon and cook for about
5 minutes, until lightly browned.
Drain on kitchen paper.

Add the potato to the pan and
cook, stirring occasionally, until
browned. Drain on kitchen paper.

Beat the eggs and cream together.
Stir in the herbs and season liberally
with salt and pepper.

When the dough has doubled in
size*, place it on a floured board and
knead thoroughly. Roll out and use
to line a 23 cm (9 inch) flan ring
placed on a baking sheet.

Spoon the onion, bacon and potato
into the case and sprinkle with the red
pepper. Pour over the egg mixture
and sprinkle with the cheese.

Bake in a preheated moderately hot
oven, 200°C (400°F), Gas Mark 6, for
20 to 25 minutes, until well risen and
golden. Serve hot or cold.
Serves 4

'TURNED-OVER' PIZZAS

1 quantity pizza dough*
oil for frying
1 quantity Tomato Sauce
(see American Hot
Pizza, below)
125 g (4 oz) matured
Cheddar cheese, diced
2 tablespoons grated
Parmesan cheese
125 g (4 oz) Italian
salami, sliced
1 tablespoon each chopped
oregano and basil
1-2 cloves garlic, crushed

When the pizza dough has risen*, divide it into 4 equal pieces and form each into a round.

Heat a little oil in a large heavy-based frying pan and fry 2 rounds at a time for about 2 to 3 minutes on each side, until golden.

Spread the hot Tomato Sauce on the pizzas, and top with the cheeses, salami, herbs and garlic. Return to the pan and cook at a lower heat for 3 minutes. Fold in half and serve immediately.
Serves 4

AMERICAN HOT PIZZA

25 g (1 oz) butter
2 onions, sliced
1 quantity pizza dough*
2-3 green chillies, seeded
and sliced lengthways
1 tablespoon each chopped
thyme and marjoram
25 g (1 oz) each Bel
Paese and Mozzarella
cheese, diced
TOMATO SAUCE:
1-2 tablespoons oil
1 clove garlic, crushed
2-3 shallots, chopped
250 g (8 oz) tomatoes,
skinned, seeded and
chopped
150 ml (¼ pint) dry
white wine
1 teaspoon dried mixed
herbs
salt and pepper
TO GARNISH (optional):
marjoram sprigs

First make the tomato sauce. Heat the oil in a pan, add the garlic and shallots and cook for about 5 minutes, until golden. Add the tomatoes, wine and mixed herbs. Bring to the boil and cook rapidly for 20 minutes, until thickened. Season with salt and pepper to taste and leave to cool.

Melt the butter in a pan, add the onions and cook for 5 minutes until golden. Leave to cool.

Roll out the dough* and slide the pizza onto a hot baking sheet*. Spread the onions on the base and cover with the tomato sauce. Sprinkle with the chillies, thyme, marjoram and cheeses.

Bake at once in a preheated hot oven, 220°C (425°F), Gas Mark 7, for 15 to 20 minutes, until the dough and topping are golden. Garnish with marjoram if liked, and serve immediately.
Serves 4

SEAFOOD PIZZA

1 quantity pizza dough*
1 quantity Tomato Sauce
(see American Hot
Pizza, opposite)
2 tomatoes, skinned and
sliced
1 × 198 g (7 oz) can
tuna fish
125 g (4 oz) peeled
prawns
squeeze of lemon juice
2 teaspoons chopped basil
25 g (1 oz) each matured
Cheddar and Bel Paese
cheese, diced

Roll out the dough* and slide onto a
hot baking sheet*. Cover with the
Tomato Sauce and place the tomatoes
around the edge. Drain and flake the
tuna fish and arrange on top with the
prawns. Squeeze over the lemon
juice. Sprinkle with the basil and
cheeses.

Bake at once in a preheated hot
oven, 220°C (425°F), Gas Mark 7, for
15 to 20 minutes, until golden. Serve
immediately, garnished with lemon
slices if preferred.
Serves 4

gr. onion / chives

ARTICHOKE AND MUSHROOM PIZZA

1 quantity pizza dough*
2 tablespoons tomato
   purée
4-6 tomatoes, skinned and
   sliced
2 tablespoons each
   chopped basil and
   oregano
1 × 397 g (14 oz) can
   artichoke hearts,
   drained and sliced
50 g (2 oz) button
   mushrooms, thinly
   sliced
3 tablespoons olive oil
25 g (1 oz) each
   Parmesan and
   matured Cheddar
   cheese, grated

Roll out the dough*. Spread the tomato purée thinly over the base. Arrange the tomatoes on top and sprinkle with the herbs. Place the artichokes and mushrooms on top and drizzle over the oil. Sprinkle with the cheeses.

Slide the pizza onto a hot baking sheet* and bake at once in a preheated hot oven, 220°C (425°F), Gas Mark 7, for 15 to 20 minutes, until golden. Serve immediately.

Serves 4

BAKED VEGETABLE PIZZA

125 g (4 oz) mangetouts
50 g (2 oz) French beans
50 g (2 oz) baby carrots,
  sliced
salt and pepper
4 canned artichoke hearts,
  drained
25 g (1 oz) butter
25 g (1 oz) flour
150 ml (¼ pint) milk
2 tablespoons cream
25 g (1 oz) Parmesan
  cheese, grated
50 g (2 oz) matured
  Cheddar cheese, grated
pinch of dried mixed herbs
2 egg yolks
1 quantity pizza dough*

Blanch the mangetouts, beans and carrots in boiling salted water for 3 minutes. Drain and leave to cool.

Cut the beans and mangetouts in half and slice the artichokes. Mix all the vegetables together and set aside.

Melt the butter in a pan, add the flour and cook for 2 minutes, without browning. Gradually add the milk, bring to the boil, stirring, and cook for 2 minutes. Remove from the heat, stir in the cream, Parmesan cheese, half the Cheddar cheese, herbs and egg yolks. Stir in the vegetables.

Roll out the dough*, making the edge at least twice as thick as the rest and 2.5 cm (1 inch) high.

Spoon the sauce into the centre and sprinkle over the remaining Cheddar cheese.

Slide the pizza onto a hot baking sheet* and bake at once in a preheated hot oven, 220°C (425°F), Gas Mark 7, for 15 to 20 minutes, until golden.

Leave for 10 minutes before serving.
Serves 4

MEAT AND CHEESE STUFFED PIZZA

4 tablespoons olive oil
1 onion, sliced
250 g (8 oz) minced beef
120 ml (4 fl oz) dry
     white wine
1-2 cloves garlic, crushed
salt and pepper
50 g (2 oz) unsmoked
     ham, diced
75 g (3 oz) matured
     Cheddar cheese, diced
50 g (2 oz) Ricotta or
     curd cheese
1 quantity pizza dough*
2 tablespoons fresh
     breadcrumbs, toasted

Heat 3 tablespoons of the oil in a pan, add the onion and cook for about 5 minutes, until golden, stirring occasionally. Add the minced beef and cook until browned, stirring constantly.

Add the wine, lower the heat slightly and cook, uncovered, for about 15 minutes, until all the liquid has reduced. Stir in the garlic, and salt and pepper to taste. Transfer to a bowl and leave to cool completely.

Stir the ham and cheeses into the mixture until very smooth.

Knead the dough on a floured board and divide into 2 unequal pieces. Roll out the larger piece into a 25 to 30 cm (10 to 12 inch) circle and place on a floured piece of circular cardboard. Sprinkle with half the breadcrumbs and cover with the filling, leaving a 1 cm (½ inch) border all round. Sprinkle with the remaining breadcrumbs and 1 tablespoon oil.

Roll out the remaining dough to the same size. Dampen the edges with water and place over the stuffing, pinching the edges together to seal well.

Brush the top with a little water and slide the pizza onto a hot baking sheet*. Bake in a preheated moderately hot oven, 200°C (400°F), Gas Mark 6, for 25 minutes or until golden.

Leave to stand for 30 to 40 minutes. Cut into wedges to serve.
Serves 4 to 6

CHILLI-TOPPED PIZZA

2 tablespoons oil
4 shallots, chopped
½-1 teaspoon chilli
   powder
250 g (8 oz) minced beef
1 × 227 g (8 oz) can
   tomatoes
dash of Tabasco sauce
1 × 213 g (7½ oz) can
   red kidney beans
1 clove garlic, crushed
salt and pepper
1 quantity pizza dough*
125 g (4 oz) Bel Paese
   cheese, diced
2 teaspoons grated
   Parmesan cheese

Heat the oil in a pan, add the shallots and cook for 2 minutes. Stir in the chilli powder and minced beef and cook until browned, stirring occasionally. Add the tomatoes, with their juice, and Tabasco.

Bring to the boil, cover and simmer for 45 minutes, until very thick, stirring occasionally. Remove from the heat.

Drain and rinse the kidney beans under cold water. Add to the pan with the garlic, and salt and pepper to taste. Leave to cool.

Roll out the dough*. Slide the pizza onto a hot baking sheet* and spoon over the chilli mixture. Sprinkle with the cheeses and bake in a preheated hot oven, 220°C (425°F), Gas Mark 7, for 15 to 20 minutes. Serve immediately.

Serves 4

HAM AND CHEESE PIZZA PIE

25 g (1 oz) butter
3 tomatoes, skinned,
    seeded and chopped
2 tablespoons dry white
    wine
6 basil leaves, finely
    chopped
salt and pepper
double quantity pizza
    dough*
125 g (4 oz) Mozzarella
    cheese, sliced
50 g (2 oz) Bel Paese
    cheese, sliced
175 g (6 oz) smoked back
    bacon, derinded and cut
    into thin strips
50 g (2 oz) matured
    Cheddar cheese, grated
beaten egg to glaze

Melt the butter in a pan, add the tomatoes and wine, bring to the boil and cook for 5 minutes. Add the basil, and salt and pepper to taste; cool.

When the dough has doubled in size*, place it on a floured board and knead thoroughly. Break off two thirds, roll out into a thin circle and use to line a greased 23 cm (9 inch) loose-bottomed cake tin, ensuring that the dough comes up the side.

Spread the tomato mixture over the base, cover with half the Mozzarella and Bel Paese and all the bacon. Lay the remaining cheese slices on top and sprinkle with the Cheddar cheese.

Roll out the remaining dough to fit the top of the pizza, dampen the edges and seal well. Leave in a warm place to rise for 30 to 40 minutes.

Brush with beaten egg and bake in a preheated moderately hot oven, 200°C (400°F), Gas Mark 6, for 15 minutes. Lower the heat to 190°C (375°F), Gas Mark 5, and cook for 20 minutes. Serve immediately.
Serves 6

FOUR SEASONS PIZZA

2 tablespoons oil
1 clove garlic, crushed
125 g (4 oz) button
   mushrooms, sliced
1 tablespoon chopped
   parsley
1-2 teaspoons capers
50 g (2 oz) peeled prawns
2 rashers streaky bacon,
   derinded and chopped
2 tablespoons sweetcorn
1 quantity pizza dough*
½ quantity Tomato Sauce
   (see American Hot
   Pizza, page 30)
125 g (4 oz) Mozzarella
   cheese, diced
2 tomatoes, sliced
4 black olives, stoned and
   halved
1 teaspoon dried mixed
   herbs

Heat the oil in a pan, add the garlic and mushrooms and cook for 2 minutes. Stir in the parsley and leave to cool.

Mix the capers and prawns together. Mix the bacon and sweetcorn together.

Roll out the dough*. Spread the Tomato Sauce over the base and sprinkle with the cheese. Using a palette knife, gently mark the pizza into quarters.

Arrange the mushrooms on one quarter, the prawns on the another, sprinkle the bacon and sweetcorn on the third quarter, and arrange the tomatoes and olives on the last quarter. Sprinkle the herbs all over.

Slide the pizza onto a hot baking sheet* and bake at once in a preheated hot oven, 220°C (425°F), Gas Mark 7, for 15 to 20 minutes, until golden. Serve immediately.
Serves 4

FRENCH BREAD PIZZA

1 French loaf
2 tablespoons oil
1 × 64 g (2¼ oz) can
  tomato purée
1 teaspoon dried mixed
  herbs
1-2 cloves garlic, crushed
3 tomatoes, sliced
175 g (6 oz) peeled
  prawns
125 g (4 oz) Mozzarella
  cheese, grated
2 teaspoons capers
125 g (4 oz) salami,
  sliced
8 stuffed olives, sliced
125 g (4 oz) Gruyère
  cheese, grated

Cut the bread in half lengthways, brush the crust with the oil, and spread the tomato purée over the cut surfaces. Sprinkle with the herbs and garlic.

Arrange the tomatoes, prawns and Mozzarella cheese on one half. Sprinkle with the capers.

Arrange the salami and olives on the other half. Sprinkle with the Gruyère cheese.

Cut each piece of bread into 4. Place on a lightly greased baking sheet and bake in a preheated moderately hot oven, 200°C (400°F), Gas Mark 6, for 12 to 15 minutes. Serve hot.
Serves 4 to 8

ASPARAGUS AND TOMATO PAN PIZZA

1 × 64 g (2¼ oz) can
  tomato purée
1 clove garlic, crushed
½ teaspoon each dried
  basil and oregano
1 quantity pizza dough*
25 g (1 oz) Mozzarella
  cheese, grated
250 g (8 oz) tomatoes,
  skinned and sliced
250 g (8 oz) frozen
  asparagus, thawed
75 g (3 oz) Bel Paese
  cheese, cubed
1 tablespoon chopped
  thyme (optional)
1 tablespoon grated
  Parmesan cheese

Mix together the tomato purée, garlic and herbs.

Lightly grease a very large heavy-based frying pan. Roll out the dough on a floured board to the size of the pan. Place in the pan and bring a little dough up the sides.

Sprinkle over the Mozzarella cheese and spoon the tomato paste mixture on top. Arrange the tomatoes and asparagus over the pizza and sprinkle with the Bel Paese, thyme, if using, and Parmesan cheese.

Cook over medium heat for 15 to 20 minutes, then place under a preheated hot grill for 1 to 2 minutes until golden. Serve immediately.
Serves 4

PIZZA TURNOVERS

1 quantity pizza dough*
olive oil for brushing
4 tomatoes, skinned,
  seeded and chopped
1 tablespoon chopped basil
6 small slices Mozzarella
  cheese
175 g (6 oz) peeled
  prawns
25 g (1 oz) matured
  Cheddar cheese, grated
salt and pepper
oil for deep-frying

Divide the dough into 6 equal pieces. Roll out each piece very thinly into a 15 cm (6 inch) circle, turning the dough to prevent shrinking. Brush the centre of each circle with a little olive oil and the edge with water.

Divide the tomatoes between the circles, placing in the centre, and sprinkle with the basil. Place a slice of Mozzarella on top, then the prawns. Sprinkle with the grated cheese and season liberally with salt and pepper.

Fold the dough over the filling to form a crescent and seal the edges well. Place on a floured board, cover with a clean tea-towel and leave to rise in a warm place for 25 to 30 minutes.

Heat the oil in a deep pan, add 2 'turnovers' at a time and cook for 5 to 6 minutes on each side, until golden. Drain on kitchen paper and serve immediately.
Serves 6

MAIN COURSE PASTA DISHES

LASAGNE WITH RICOTTA PESTO

200 g (7 oz) basil leaves
175 ml (6 fl oz) olive oil
75 g (3 oz) pinenuts
4 cloves garlic, roughly chopped
175 g (6 oz) Parmesan cheese, grated
25 g (1 oz) matured Cheddar cheese, grated
50 g (2 oz) Ricotta or curd cheese
salt
50 g (2 oz) butter, softened
250 g (8 oz) quantity pasta dough*
basil sprigs to garnish

Put the basil, oil, pinenuts and garlic in an electric blender or food processor and work until smooth. Transfer to a bowl and stir in the cheeses and salt to taste. Beat in the butter.

Cut the pasta into 7.5 × 13 cm (3 × 5 inch) lengths and cook, in two batches, for about 1 minute, until *al dente**. Drain and keep warm.

Add 1 tablespoon of the cooking water to the pesto and mix well.

Arrange a quarter of the lasagne on a warmed serving dish and cover with a quarter of the pesto. Repeat the layers. Garnish with basil and serve immediately.

Serves 4 to 6

SPAGHETTI ALLA CARBONARA

500 g (1 lb) fresh
  spaghetti
125 g (4 oz) bacon,
  derinded and chopped
50 g (2 oz) butter
2 cloves garlic, crushed
3 eggs
142 ml (5 fl oz) double
  cream
75 g (3 oz) matured
  Cheddar cheese, grated
50 g (2 oz) Parmesan
  cheese, grated
1 teaspoon French
  mustard
salt and pepper
1 tablespoon each chopped
  thyme and parsley
thyme sprigs to garnish

Cook the spaghetti until *al dente**.
Meanwhile fry the bacon in its own
fat until crisp. Drain the pasta
thoroughly, return to the pan, add
the butter and toss well. Stir in the
garlic and bacon.

Beat together the eggs, cream,
cheeses and mustard. Season with a
little salt and plenty of pepper and add
the herbs.

Pour the mixture over the spaghetti
and stir over a gentle heat until the
sauce is creamy, taking care not to
'scramble' the eggs. Transfer to a
warmed serving dish and garnish
with thyme. Serve immediately,
accompanied by Parmesan cheese.
Serves 4 to 6

PASTA AND SPINACH ROLL

75 g (3 oz) butter
1 large onion, chopped
50 g (2 oz) Parma ham, diced
500 g (1 lb) frozen leaf spinach, roughly chopped
200 g (7 oz) Ricotta or curd cheese
60 g (2½ oz) Parmesan cheese, grated
little grated nutmeg
1 egg yolk
250 g (8 oz) quantity pasta dough*
300 ml (½ pint) Béchamel sauce (see Baked Rigatoni, page 53)

TOMATO SAUCE:
1 tablespoon olive oil
1 large onion, finely chopped
2 carrots, chopped
2 celery sticks, chopped
1 × 397 g (14 oz) can tomatoes
150 ml (¼ pint) dry white wine
½ teaspoon dried mixed herbs
salt and pepper

First, make the tomato sauce. Heat the olive oil in a pan, add the onion, carrots and celery and cook for 5 minutes, without browning, stirring occasionally. Add the tomatoes and their juice, the wine, herbs, and salt and pepper to taste. Bring to the boil, cover and simmer for 20 minutes. Remove the lid and cook for 10 to 15 minutes until thickened; set aside.

Melt the butter in a pan, add the onion and cook until golden brown. Lower the heat, stir in the ham and spinach and cook for 5 minutes, stirring occasionally.

Put the Ricotta or curd cheese and all but 2 tablespoons of the Parmesan cheese in a bowl. Stir in the spinach mixture, and season with salt and pepper to taste. Add the nutmeg and egg yolk.

Roll out the pasta to an oblong shape and cover with the filling, leaving a 2.5 cm (1 inch) border around the edge. Fold in the two ends and roll up like a Swiss roll. Wrap in muslin and tie the ends securely with string.

Cook in boiling salted water for 20 minutes. Remove from the pan, leave to cool then remove the muslin.

Stir the Béchamel sauce into the tomato sauce.

Slice the roll into 1.5 cm (¾ inch) thick slices and arrange in a buttered ovenproof dish. Spoon over the sauce and sprinkle with the reserved Parmesan cheese.

Bake uncovered in a preheated moderately hot oven, 200°C (400°F), Gas Mark 6, for 15 to 20 minutes. Garnish with fresh herbs if liked, and serve immediately.

Serves 4 to 6

NOTE: if you do not have a large enough pan, make 2 smaller rolls.

PASTA WITH SQUID AND TOMATO

350 g (12 oz) squid, cut
    into 5 mm (¼ inch)
    strips
150 ml (¼ pint) dry
    white wine
1 bouquet garni
6 tablespoons olive oil
1 large onion, chopped
750 g (1½ lb) tomatoes,
    skinned, seeded and
    chopped
2 tablespoons chopped
    basil
1 tablespoon chopped
    parsley
salt and pepper
1-2 cloves garlic, crushed
500 g (1 lb) fresh
    tagliatelle
25 g (1 oz) butter
parsley sprigs to garnish

Place the squid in a shallow pan with
the wine and bouquet garni. Bring to
the boil, cover and simmer for
2 minutes. Using a slotted spoon,
remove the squid and set aside.
Discard the bouquet garni. Reserve
the cooking liquid.

Heat the oil in a pan, add the onion
and cook for 5 minutes, without
browning. Stir in the tomatoes,
herbs, and salt and pepper to taste.
Strain the reserved liquid into the
pan, bring to the boil, cover and
simmer for 30 minutes. Add the
garlic and boil, for about 5 minutes,
until reduced and thickened.

Meanwhile, cook the tagliatelle
until al dente*. Drain thoroughly and
turn into a warmed serving dish. Add
the butter and toss well. Add the
squid to the sauce, heat through, pour
over the pasta and serve immediately,
garnished with parsley.
Serves 4 to 6

PASTA WITH BABY VEGETABLES

3 tablespoons dry white
  wine
1 tablespoon chopped
  chervil
2 tablespoons double
  cream
175 g (6 oz) butter
125 g (4 oz) mushrooms,
  sliced
2 tomatoes, skinned,
  seeded and chopped
salt and pepper
1 teaspoon lemon juice
2 tablespoons olive oil
150 g (5 oz) cauliflower
  florets
1 small courgette, thinly
  sliced
50 g (2 oz) mangetouts
4 canned artichoke hearts,
  drained and quartered
50 g (2 oz) peas
350 g (12 oz) dried
  spaghetti

Put the wine and chervil in a pan, bring to the boil and boil steadily until reduced by half. Add the cream, 150 g (5 oz) of the butter in small pieces, the mushrooms and tomatoes. Season well with salt and pepper. Bring to the boil and boil for 30 seconds. Stir in the lemon juice.

Heat the olive oil in a large frying pan or wok, add all the remaining vegetables and stir-fry for 2 to 3 minutes.

Meanwhile, cook the spaghetti until *al dente**. Drain well and toss in the remaining butter. Spoon over the mushroom sauce and toss well.

Transfer to a warmed serving plate, surround with the vegetables and serve immediately.
Serves 4

TORTELLINI WITH RICOTTA AND SPINACH SAUCE

125 g (4 oz) butter
250 g (8 oz) frozen leaf
  spinach, thawed and
  chopped
salt and pepper
500 g (1 lb) fresh
  tortellini
125 g (4 oz) Ricotta or
  curd cheese
50 g (2 oz) Parmesan
  cheese, grated

Heat half the butter in a large frying pan, add the spinach and toss thoroughly. Season well with salt and pepper. Sauté the spinach for 2 minutes, stirring constantly.

Cook the tortellini until *al dente**. Drain thoroughly and toss in the remaining butter.

Stir the Ricotta cheese and half of the Parmesan into the spinach mixture, then stir in the pasta. Transfer to a warmed serving dish, sprinkle with the remaining Parmesan and serve immediately.
Serves 4

CHICKEN AND NUTS WITH NOODLES

500 g (1 lb) chicken breast
2 tablespoons soy sauce
4 tablespoons dry sherry
125 g (4 oz) unsalted
    peanuts
3 tablespoons oil
1 bunch spring onions,
    chopped
2 cloves garlic, thinly
    sliced
1 cm (½ inch) piece fresh
    root ginger, chopped
3 tablespoons Hoi Sin
    sauce (Chinese plum
    sauce)
350 g (12 oz) dried
    vermicelli
salt
spring onions to garnish

Cut the chicken into 2.5 cm (1 inch) pieces. Place in a bowl, pour over the soy sauce and sherry and mix well. Cover and leave for 30 minutes.

Put the nuts on a baking tray and place in a preheated moderate oven, 180°C (350°F), Gas Mark 4, for 8 to 10 minutes until brown.

Heat the oil in a wok or large frying pan, add the spring onions, garlic and ginger and cook, without browning, for 1 minute. Add the chicken and marinade, increase the heat and cook for 10 to 12 minutes, stirring occasionally. Stir in the Hoi Sin sauce.

Cook the vermicelli until *al dente**; drain thoroughly. Add to the pan and cook for a further 2 minutes. Transfer to a warmed serving dish and serve immediately, garnished with spring onions.
Serves 4

TRADITIONAL MACARONI CHEESE

250 g (8 oz) dried short-
  cut macaroni
50 g (2 oz) butter
25 g (1 oz) plain flour
450 ml (¾ pint) milk
1 heaped teaspoon English
  mustard
dash of Tabasco sauce
dash of Worcestershire
  sauce
175 g (6 oz) matured
  Cheddar cheese, grated
25 g (1 oz) dried
  breadcrumbs
25 g (1 oz) Parmesan
  cheese, grated
2 tomatoes, sliced

Cook the macaroni until *al dente**;
drain thoroughly, then toss in half the
butter.

Heat the remaining butter in a pan,
stir in the flour and cook, stirring, for
2 minutes, without browning.
Gradually add the milk and bring to
the boil, stirring constantly. Cook for
2 minutes, then stir in the mustard,
and Tabasco and Worcestershire
sauces. Add the Cheddar cheese and
stir until melted. Fold in the
macaroni.

Spoon into a buttered ovenproof
dish and sprinkle with the
breadcrumbs and Parmesan cheese.

Bake in a preheated moderately hot
oven, 200°C (400°F), Gas Mark 6, for
25 to 30 minutes. Arrange the tomato
slices on top, return to the oven for
5 to 10 minutes, until hot and golden
brown. Serve immediately.
Serves 4

GARLIC CHICKEN WITH NOODLES

2 tablespoons oil
75 g (3 oz) butter
1 large onion, finely
  chopped
500 g (1 lb) boneless
  chicken breasts
2-3 garlic bulbs, broken
  into cloves
300 ml (½ pint) dry
  white wine
1 teaspoon chopped
  tarragon
salt and pepper
125 g (4 oz) button
  mushrooms, sliced
4 tablespoons chopped
  parsley
500 g (1 lb) fresh
  tagliatelle verdi or
  noodles
25 g (1 oz) dried
  breadcrumbs
25 g (1 oz) Parmesan
  cheese, grated
tarragon sprigs to garnish

Heat the oil and 50 g (2 oz) of the butter in a pan, add the onion and cook for 2 minutes, until transparent.

Cut the chicken into 5 cm (2 inch) pieces, add to the pan and brown on all sides. Add the garlic, wine, tarragon, and salt and pepper to taste, bring to the boil, cover and simmer for 30 minutes. Remove the garlic, stir in the mushrooms and cook for 2 minutes. Stir in the parsley.

Cook the pasta until *al dente**; drain thoroughly and toss in the remaining butter.

Mix the sauce and noodles together, spoon into a buttered ovenproof dish, and sprinkle with the breadcrumbs and Parmesan cheese. Bake in a preheated moderately hot oven, 200°C (400°F), Gas Mark 6, for 20 to 25 minutes, until hot and golden brown.

Garnish with tarragon, and serve immediately.

Serves 4 to 6

PASTA WITH CHICKEN LIVERS

1 tablespoon oil
50 g (2 oz) butter
4 shallots, chopped
4 rashers back bacon,
    derinded and chopped
250 g (8 oz) minced beef
150 ml (¼ pint) each dry
    vermouth and dry white
    wine
350 g (12 oz) tomatoes,
    skinned, seeded and
    chopped
salt and pepper
2 cloves garlic, crushed
2 tablespoons each
    chopped parsley,
    marjoram and sage
250 g (8 oz) chicken
    livers, chopped
500 g (1 lb) dried pasta
    spirals or shells

Heat the oil and half the butter in a pan, add the shallots and cook, stirring constantly, for 2 to 3 minutes, without browning. Add the bacon and minced beef, increase the heat and brown quickly, stirring.

Add the vermouth and wine and boil rapidly for 15 minutes. Stir in the tomatoes and season well with salt and pepper. Stir in the garlic and herbs. Add the chicken livers and cook for 3 minutes.

Cook the pasta until *al dente**. Drain thoroughly, turn into a warmed serving dish, add the remaining butter and toss well.

Spoon the sauce over the pasta and toss well. Garnish with sage or parsley if liked, and serve immediately.
Serves 6

NOODLES WITH BROCCOLI, MUSHROOMS AND SHELLFISH

1 head of broccoli
2 tablespoons olive oil
1 tablespoon chopped fresh
    ginger
2 cloves garlic, thinly
    sliced
125 g (4 oz) button
    mushrooms, sliced
250 g (8 oz) scallops
175 g (6 oz) peeled
    prawns
150 ml (¼ pint) dry
    sherry
284 ml (½ pint) double
    cream
1 teaspoon each chopped
    marjoram and thyme
1 tablespoon parsley
salt and pepper
500 g (1 lb) fresh
    tagliatelle verdi

Break the broccoli into florets and cook for 1 minute; leave to cool.

Heat the oil in a wok or large frying pan, add the ginger and garlic and brown lightly. Stir in the mushrooms, scallops and prawns. Pour over the sherry. Boil rapidly until the liquid has reduced to about 2 tablespoons. Add the cream, herbs, and salt and pepper to taste.

Meanwhile, cook the tagliatelle until al dente*; drain thoroughly.

Add the broccoli to the sauce, check the seasoning and heat through.

Transfer the tagliatelle to a warmed serving dish, pour over the sauce and serve immediately.
Serves 4 to 6

SPAGHETTI AL TONNO

4 tablespoons olive oil
2-3 cloves garlic, crushed
1 kg (2 lb) tomatoes,
    skinned, seeded and
    chopped
1 tablespoon each chopped
    basil and oregano
salt and pepper
2 × 198 g (7 oz) cans
    tuna fish, drained and
    flaked
1 teaspoon anchovy
    essence
2 teaspoons capers
    (optional)
500 g (1 lb) fresh
    spaghetti
25 g (1 oz) butter
oregano or basil sprigs to
    garnish (optional)

Heat the oil in a pan, add the garlic and cook until golden brown, stirring occasionally. Add the tomatoes, herbs, and pepper to taste. Bring to the boil and simmer, uncovered, for 30 minutes, until thickened. Add the tuna, anchovy essence and capers, if using.

Cook the spaghetti until al dente*. Drain thoroughly, turn into a warmed serving dish, add the butter and toss well.

Taste the sauce and add salt if necessary, then spoon over the pasta. Garnish with oregano or basil if liked, and serve immediately.
Serves 4 to 6

SPAGHETTI WITH MUSSELS

1 kg (2 lb) fresh mussels
4 tablespoons olive oil
75 g (3 oz) butter
2-3 cloves garlic, crushed
1 large onion, finely
  chopped
750 g (1½ lb) tomatoes,
  skinned, seeded and
  chopped
150 ml (¼ pint) dry
  white wine
1 teaspoon dried mixed
  herbs
salt and pepper
500 g (1 lb) fresh
  spaghetti
chopped parsley to garnish

Put the mussels in a large pan, cover
with water, bring to the boil and
cook for 5 to 6 minutes, until the
shells have opened. Reserve 4 tablespoons water. Drain the mussels,
discarding any that have not opened.

Heat the oil and 25 g (1 oz) of the
butter in a pan, add the garlic and
onion and cook for 5 minutes, until
pale golden. Add the tomatoes, wine,
herbs, salt and pepper to taste, and
the reserved cooking liquid. Bring to
the boil and cook, uncovered, for
30 minutes, until thickened.

Meanwhile, cook the spaghetti
until *al dente**. Drain thoroughly and
turn into a warmed serving dish. Add
the remaining butter and toss well.

Add the mussels to the sauce and
heat through. Pour over the pasta,
sprinkle with chopped parsley and
serve immediately.
Serves 4 to 6

BAKED RIGATONI WITH MEAT SAUCE

2 tablespoons oil
50 g (2 oz) butter
1 onion, chopped
2 celery sticks, chopped
2 carrots, chopped
350 g (12 oz) minced beef
salt and pepper
300 ml (½ pint) dry
    white wine
6 tablespoons milk
little grated nutmeg
1-2 cloves garlic, crushed
1 × 397 g (14 oz) can
    tomatoes, chopped
500 g (1 lb) dried rigatoni
    or penne
40 g (1½ oz) butter
6 tablespoons grated
    Parmesan cheese
BECHAMEL SAUCE:
450 ml (¾ pint) milk
1 carrot
1 onion
3-4 peppercorns
1 bay leaf
50 g (2 oz) butter
50 g (2 oz) plain flour

Heat the oil and butter in a pan, add the onion, celery and carrots and cook for 2 minutes, without browning. Increase the heat, add the minced beef and brown well. Season liberally with salt and pepper, add the wine and cook rapidly until it has evaporated.

Lower the heat, add the milk and cook until it has reduced completely.

Stir in the nutmeg, garlic and tomatoes with their juice. Cover and simmer for 1 to 1½ hours, stirring occasionally. Check the seasoning.

Meanwhile, make the Béchamel sauce. Put the milk, carrot, onion, peppercorns and bay leaf in a pan and bring to the boil slowly. Turn off the heat, leave to cool, then stain.

Melt the butter in a pan, add the flour and cook for 1 minute, without browning. Gradually add the strained milk, stirring constantly. Bring to the boil and cook for 2 minutes. Season with salt and pepper to taste.

Cook the pasta until just *al dente**. Drain, place in a large bowl with the butter and toss well. Pour over the meat and Béchamel sauces, and 4 tablespoons of the Parmesan cheese; mix well.

Transfer to a buttered ovenproof dish, sprinkle with the remaining cheese and bake in a preheated moderately hot oven, 200°C (400°F), Gas Mark 6, for 20 to 25 minutes until hot and golden brown. Serve immediately.
Serves 6

CAPPELLETTI WITH FISH STUFFING AND SHRIMP SAUCE

1 small onion, halved
1 celery stick, roughly
  chopped
1 small carrot, roughly
  chopped
350 g (12 oz) sea bass or
  other white fish, skin
  removed
175 ml (6 fl oz) dry white
  wine
salt and pepper
2 egg yolks
20 g (¾ oz) Parmesan
  cheese, grated
1 teaspoon chopped
  marjoram
pinch of grated nutmeg
250 g (8 oz) quantity
  pasta dough*
25 g (1 oz) butter
SAUCE:
4 tablespoons olive oil
2 cloves garlic, crushed
8 tomatoes, skinned,
  seeded and chopped
4 tablespoons dry white
  wine
250 g (8 oz) peeled
  prawns, chopped
284 ml (½ pint) double
  cream
2 tablespoons chopped
  parsley
TO GARNISH:
parsley and marjoram
  sprigs

Put the onion, celery, carrot and fish in a frying pan, pour over the wine and season well with salt and pepper. Bring to the boil and simmer for 10 to 12 minutes, until the fish is tender. Drain and flake the fish into a bowl. Add the egg yolks, cheese, marjoram and nutmeg. Mix well and season with salt and pepper to taste.

Cut the pasta dough into 3.5 cm (1½ inch) squares. Place ½ teaspoon of filling in the centre of each square and dampen the edges of the dough with water. With one corner facing you, fold into a triangle and seal the edges. Then take the left and right corners together to form a circle and pinch to seal. Place the cappelletti on a clean dry tea-towel and leave to dry for 1 hour.

Meanwhile, make the sauce. Put the oil and garlic in a pan and cook for 2 to 3 minutes, until the garlic is golden brown. Add the tomatoes and wine, bring to the boil and simmer, uncovered, for 15 to 20 minutes, until thickened. Stir in the prawns and season with salt and pepper to taste.

Add the cream and gradually bring to the boil, stirring constantly. Stir in the parsley and remove from the heat.

Cook the cappelletti for 30 seconds to 1 minute, until *al dente**. Drain thoroughly and transfer to a warmed serving dish. Add the butter, toss well, then pour over the sauce. Garnish with parsley and marjoram and serve immediately.
Serves 4

SEAFOOD PASTA

4 fillets of sole, skinned,
  with bones
300 ml (½ pint) dry
  white wine
1 small onion, halved
½ teaspoon dried mixed
  herbs
50 g (2 oz) butter
1 clove garlic, crushed
2 shallots, chopped
6 large scallops
4 large tomatoes, skinned,
  seeded and chopped
1 teaspoon chopped basil
2 tablespoons chopped
  parsley
142 ml (5 fl oz) double
  cream
salt and pepper
500 g (1 lb) fresh egg
  noodles or tagliatelle
250 g (8 oz) peeled
  prawns
whole prawns to garnish

Place the skin and bones from the
fish in a pan with the wine, onion and
herbs. Simmer, uncovered, for
20 minutes. Cool and strain.

Melt half the butter in a pan, add
the garlic and shallots and cook for
5 minutes. Cut the fish into 5 cm
(2 inch) pieces and add to the pan
with the fish stock. Bring to the boil,
simmer for 2 minutes, remove the
fish and set aside. Add the white part
of the scallops and cook for 30
seconds, add the coral part and cook
for just under 30 seconds; remove.

Boil the liquid until reduced to
2 tablespoons. Add the tomatoes and
basil and cook for 10 minutes, stirring
occasionally, until thickened. Stir in
the parsley, cream, and salt and
pepper to taste.

Cook the noodles until *al dente**.
Drain and turn into a warmed serving
dish. Add the remaining butter and
toss well. Add the prawns and fish to
the sauce, bring to the boil, then pour
over the noodles. Serve immediately,
garnished with whole prawns.
Serves 4

HAM AND MUSHROOM LASAGNE

4 tablespoons oil
75 g (3 oz) butter
1 small onion, chopped
300 ml (½ pint) dry
   white wine
3 large tomatoes, skinned,
   seeded and chopped
750 g (1½ lb) button
   mushrooms, sliced
1-2 cloves garlic, crushed
1 teaspoon dried mixed
   herbs
2 tablespoons chopped
   parsley
salt and pepper
300 g (10 oz) dried
   lasagne
450 ml (¾ pint)
   Béchamel sauce (see
   Baked Rigatoni,
   page 53)
350 g (12 oz) unsmoked
   ham, in thin strips
1 × 397 g (14 oz) can
   artichoke hearts,
   drained and sliced
50 g (2 oz) Parmesan
   cheese, grated

Heat the oil and butter in a pan, add the onion and cook for 2 minutes. Add the wine and tomatoes, bring to the boil and simmer for 20 minutes, stirring occasionally, until the liquid has evaporated.

Stir in the mushrooms, garlic and herbs and cook for 6 to 7 minutes, until thickened. Add the parsley, and salt and pepper to taste.

Cook the lasagne until *al dente**. Drain and cool under cold running water, then drain thoroughly.

Line the base of a large buttered ovenproof dish with lasagne. Spoon over some mushrooms, then a little Béchamel sauce. Sprinkle with ham and artichoke. Repeat the layers, finishing with pasta and Béchamel sauce.

Sprinkle with the Parmesan and bake in a preheated moderately hot oven, 200°C (400°F), Gas Mark 6 for 20 to 25 minutes until golden brown. Serve immediately.
Serves 6

SALAD ACCOMPANIMENTS

AVOCADO AND MUSHROOM SALAD

250 g (8 oz) button
mushrooms, sliced
½ head of curly endive
1 lime or lemon
2 large avocado pears
25 g (1 oz) pinenuts,
toasted
DRESSING:
6 tablespoons olive oil
3-4 tablespoons lime juice
1 teaspoon finely grated
lemon rind
1 clove garlic, crushed
1 teaspoon crushed
coriander seeds
1 teaspoon honey
salt and pepper

Mix the dressing ingredients together, seasoning with salt and pepper to taste. Put the mushrooms in a large bowl, pour over the dressing and toss well, until all the mushrooms are coated.

Arrange the endive on a flat plate. Squeeze the juice from half of the lime or lemon; slice the remainder. Slice the avocados and sprinkle with the lime or lemon juice to prevent browning. Arrange on top of the endive.

Spoon the mushrooms in the centre. Sprinkle the pinenuts over the salad, and garnish with the lime or lemon slices. Serve immediately.
Serves 4

COUNTRY GARDEN SALAD

250 g (8 oz) very small
  new potatoes
salt and pepper
mint sprig
250 g (8 oz) new carrots,
  quartered lengthways
250 g (8 oz) peas
125 g (4 oz) small French
  beans
1 thin leek, sliced
DRESSING:
4 tablespoons olive oil
2 tablespoons lemon juice
1 teaspoon Dijon mustard
1/2 teaspoon honey
1 clove garlic, crushed
2 tablespoons chopped
  mint

Cook the potatoes in boiling salted water with a sprig of mint for 10 to 12 minutes, until tender. Drain and cool under running cold water. Drain thoroughly.

Cook the carrots in boiling salted water for 7 to 10 minutes, add the peas and French beans to the pan and cook for a further 3 minutes. Drain the vegetables and cool under running cold water. Drain thoroughly.

Put the cooked vegetables in a large bowl and add the leek.

Mix the dressing ingredients together, seasoning with salt and pepper to taste. Spoon over the vegetables and mix well.

Pile the salad into a salad bowl and serve immediately.

Serves 4

FRENCH BEAN AND HAZELNUT SALAD

500 g (1 lb) small French
  beans
salt and pepper
50 g (2 oz) shelled
  hazelnuts
few lettuce leaves
DRESSING:
1 teaspoon Dijon mustard
finely grated rind of
  1/2 lemon
juice of 1 lemon
7-8 tablespoons double
  cream, lightly whipped

Cook the beans in boiling salted water for 4 to 5 minutes, until just tender. Drain, cool under cold running water. Drain thoroughly. Cut the hazelnuts into thin slices. Place under a moderate grill until golden.

Mix the dressing ingredients together in a large bowl, add the beans and toss well. Season with salt and pepper to taste.

Arrange the lettuce on a serving dish. Pile the beans in the centre and sprinkle over the nuts. Garnish with fresh herbs as liked, and serve immediately.

Serves 4

CONTINENTAL SUMMER SALAD

4 carrots, grated
1 tablespoon chopped
  parsley
2 small fennel bulbs, sliced
juice of 1/2 lemon
1 tablespoon chopped
  thyme
2 large tomatoes
125 g (4 oz) Mozzarella
  cheese
175 g (6 oz) spinach
1 head of radicchio
50 g (2 oz) salted cashew
  nuts
DRESSING:
6 tablespoons olive oil
3 tablespoons lemon juice
1 teaspoon each grated
  lemon rind, French
  mustard and honey
1-2 cloves garlic, crushed
3 tablespoons chopped
  basil
salt and pepper

Mix together the carrots and parsley and set aside.

Mix the fennel, lemon juice and thyme together.

Arrange the carrots on one quarter of a large platter, the fennel on the next quarter.

Slice the tomatoes and Mozzarella and arrange alternately in the third quarter.

Tear the spinach and radicchio leaves into pieces and arrange on the remaining quarter of the platter. Sprinkle with the nuts.

Mix the dressing ingredients together, seasoning with salt and pepper to taste. Spoon over the salad and serve immediately.

Serves 4

NOTE: This dish is also suitable to serve as an hors d'oeuvre.

COURGETTE AND BACON SALAD

500 g (1 lb) baby
  courgettes
2 spring onions
175 g (6 oz) streaky
  bacon, derinded
2 hard-boiled egg yolks,
  sieved
DRESSING:
6 tablespoons olive oil
3 tablespoons lemon juice
1 teaspoon honey
1 teaspoon coarse grain
  mustard
1-2 cloves garlic, crushed
2 tablespoons each
  chopped marjoram and
  thyme
salt and pepper
TO GARNISH (optional):
marjoram and thyme
  sprigs

Slice the courgettes very thinly and
arrange on a plate. Chop the spring
onions finely and sprinkle on top.

Mix the dressing ingredients
together, seasoning with salt and
pepper to taste. Spoon over the
courgettes and set aside.

Grill the bacon until crisp and
golden brown, cool and crumble into
pieces.

Sprinkle the egg yolk and bacon
over the salad, garnish with
marjoram and thyme sprigs if liked,
and serve immediately.

Serves 4

MOZZARELLA SALAD

3 large tomatoes
¼ cucumber
1 red and 1 green pepper,
  cored and seeded
2-3 young courgettes
250 g (8 oz) Mozzarella
  cheese
4 spring onions, chopped
DRESSING:
6 tablespoons olive oil
3-4 tablespoons lime juice
1-2 cloves garlic, crushed
1 teaspoon each honey and
  French mustard
1 tablespoon each chopped
  parsley, basil and
  majoram
1-2 teaspoons green
  peppercorns (optional)
salt
TO GARNISH :
basil sprigs

Thinly slice the tomatoes, cucumber, peppers, courgettes and cheese and arrange on a flat serving platter, as illustrated. Sprinkle with the spring onions.

Mix the dressing ingredients together, seasoning with salt to taste. Spoon over the salad, cover and chill for 30 minutes. Remove from the refrigerator 15 minutes before required.

Garnish with basil sprigs to serve.
Serves 4 to 6

CLASSIC GREEN SALAD

1 small lettuce
1/4 cucumber, sliced
1 green pepper, cored,
    seeded and sliced
1 bunch watercress
4 spring onions, chopped
2 celery sticks, chopped
1 head of chicory, chopped
2 tablespoons each
    chopped thyme and
    marjoram
little mustard and cress
DRESSING:
50 g (2 oz) each
    Roquefort, Stilton and
    cream cheese
150 g (5 oz) natural
    yogurt
2 tablespoons mayonnaise
dash of Tabasco sauce
salt and pepper
2 tablespoons snipped
    chives

First, make the dressing. Cream the cheeses together in a mixing bowl, then gradually stir in the yogurt and mayonnaise. Add the Tabasco, and season with salt and pepper to taste. Stir in the chives. If the dressing is too thick, add a little cold water.

Tear the lettuce into pieces and arrange in a large salad bowl with the cucumber, pepper and watercress. Chop the spring onions, celery and chicory and add to the salad bowl; toss well. Sprinkle over the herbs and spoon sufficient dressing onto the salad to coat it lightly.

Sprinkle with the mustard and cress and serve immediately.
Serves 4 to 6
NOTE: Any remaining dressing will keep in the refrigerator for 4 to 5 days in a covered container.

FRENCH VEGETABLE SALAD

250 g (8 oz) mangetouts
125 g (4 oz) young
   French beans
salt and pepper
1 fennel bulb
3 tablespoons lemon juice
4 tomatoes, quartered
¼ cucumber, diced
250 g (8 oz) peeled
   prawns
few stuffed olives
DRESSING:
1-2 cloves garlic, crushed
½ teaspoon Dijon
   mustard
dash each of Tabasco and
   Worcestershire sauce
6 tablespoons mayonnaise
6 anchovy fillets, finely
   chopped
1 tablespoon each chopped
   parsley and chives

Blanch the mangetouts and beans for 2 minutes in boiling salted water. Drain and cool under cold running water. Drain thoroughly.

Slice the fennel and toss in the lemon juice; set aside a few feathery leaves for garnish.

Put the mangetouts, beans, tomatoes, and fennel with the lemon juice in a large bowl. Stir in the cucumber and prawns.

Mix the dressing ingredients together, seasoning with salt and pepper to taste. Pour over the salad and toss well.

Pile the salad in a bowl, garnish with the stuffed olives and fennel leaves and serve immediately.
Serves 4

ITALIAN CAULIFLOWER SALAD

1 large cauliflower
4 spring onions
125 g (4 oz) Italian
   salami, diced
125 g (4 oz) Mortadella,
   diced
25 g (1 oz) black olives
DRESSING:
2 tomatoes
1 canned pimiento
4 tablespoons mayonnaise
1 clove garlic, crushed
   (optional)
6-8 green olives, stoned
   and chopped
salt and pepper
TO GARNISH (optional):
marjoram sprigs

Break the cauliflower into small florets and chop the spring onions. Place in a bowl with the salami and Mortadella.

To make the dressing, skin, seed and chop the tomatoes, and finely chop the pimiento. Put the mayonnaise in a bowl, stir in the tomatoes, pimiento, garlic, if using, and green olives, and season with salt and pepper to taste. Spoon over the salad and mix well.

Arrange in a serving dish, sprinkle with the black olives and garnish with marjoram sprigs if available.
Serves 4

ENDIVE AND BACON SALAD

175 g (6 oz) streaky
    bacon, derinded
3 thick slices stale bread
oil for deep-frying
1 large head of curly
    endive
2 heads of radicchio
1-2 avocado pears
juice of 1 lemon
1-2 hard-boiled eggs
1 tablespoon chopped
    parsley
DRESSING:
6 tablespoons olive oil
3 tablespoons lemon juice
1-2 teaspoons coarse grain
    mustard
1-2 cloves garlic, crushed
1 teaspoon honey
salt and pepper

Grill the bacon until crisp and golden
brown, cool and crumble into pieces.

Remove the crusts, then cut the
bread into cubes or rounds. Heat the
oil in a pan, add the croûtons and fry
until golden brown. Drain on kitchen
paper.

Separate the endive and radicchio
into leaves, tear into pieces and place
in a deep bowl. Roughly chop the
avocado and toss in the lemon juice.
Drain and add to the salad with the
bacon and croûtons.

Chop the egg white, sieve the yolk,
and sprinkle over the salad.

Mix the dressing ingredients
together, seasoning with salt and
pepper to taste, pour over the salad
and toss well. Sprinkle with the
parsley and serve immediately.
Serves 4

65

TUNA AND BEAN SALAD

1 × 425 g (15 oz) can red
    kidney beans
1 × 425 g (15 oz) can
    cannellini beans
2-3 celery sticks
2-3 large spring onions
2 heads of radicchio
1 × 198 g (7 oz) can tuna
    fish, drained and flaked
1 bunch watercress
2 large slices stale bread
oil for deep-frying
DRESSING:
6 tablespoons olive oil
3 tablespoons lime or
    lemon juice
1-2 cloves garlic, crushed
1 teaspoon honey
2 tablespoons snipped
    chives
2 tablespoons chopped
    parsley
salt and pepper

Drain the beans, rinse in a colander under cold running water and drain well. Place in a bowl.

Thinly slice the celery, chop the spring onions, and tear the radicchio leaves into pieces. Add to the beans with the tuna fish.

Mix the dressing ingredients together, seasoning with salt and pepper to taste. Pour over the salad and mix well.

Arrange the watercress in a serving dish and spoon the salad into the centre.

Remove the crusts and cut the bread into cubes or crescent shapes, using small cutters. Heat the oil in a pan, add the croûtons and fry until golden. Drain on kitchen paper. Sprinkle over the salad and serve immediately.
Serves 4

RED AND WHITE COLESLAW

¼ white cabbage
¼ red cabbage
3 celery sticks
2 shallots, diced
2 large red apples
juice of 1 lemon
75 g (3 oz) dates, stoned
  and chopped
25 g (1 oz) walnuts,
  roughly chopped
25 g (1 oz) flaked
  almonds, toasted
50 g (2 oz) salted cashew
  nuts
1 tablespoon chopped
  coriander or parsley
DRESSING:
6 tablespoons mayonnaise
2 teaspoons lemon juice
1 teaspoon finely grated
  lemon rind
1 teaspoon green
  peppercorn mustard
1 tablespoon each chopped
  parsley and chives
1 clove garlic, crushed
salt

Finely shred the cabbage and thinly slice the celery. Mix the cabbage, celery and shallots together in a large bowl.

Core and slice the apples, toss in the lemon juice, then drain. Stir the apple into the salad. Add the dates and nuts and mix well.

Mix the dressing ingredients together, seasoning with salt to taste. Pile the salad into a large serving bowl and stir in the dressing. Sprinkle with the chopped coriander or parsley.

Garnish with coriander or parsley leaves if liked, and serve immediately.
Serves 4 to 6

PASTA SALADS

These salads can be served as main courses, starters, or accompaniments to grilled meat or fish. Follow the serving guide for each recipe accordingly, ie serving as a main course to the smaller number.

HERBY MACARONI SALAD

500 g (1 lb) dried
  macaroni
1 red pepper, cored, seeded
  and diced
½ cucumber, diced
150 g (5 oz) natural
  yogurt
1-2 cloves garlic, crushed
1 tablespoon each chopped
  parsley, basil, thyme,
  tarragon, chives, mint
  and dill
175 g (6 oz) streaky
  bacon, derinded
50 g (2 oz) salted peanuts

Cook the macaroni until *al dente**. Drain and cool quickly under running cold water. Drain thoroughly and place in a large bowl. Stir in the red pepper, cucumber, yogurt, garlic and herbs. Transfer to a salad bowl.

Fry the bacon in its own fat until crisp, then chop into pieces and sprinkle over the salad with the peanuts.

Garnish with herbs sprigs if liked, and serve immediately.
Serves 4 to 6

PRAWN, AVOCADO AND PASTA SALAD

500 g (1 lb) peeled
   prawns
300 g (10 oz) dried pasta
   twists
2 avocado pears, sliced
1 tablespoon each chopped
   thyme, majoram, basil
   and parsley
DRESSING:
1 clove garlic, crushed
1/2 teaspoon French
   mustard
6 tablespoons olive oil
3 tablespoons lemon juice
1 teaspoon finely grated
   lemon rind
1 teaspoon honey
salt and pepper
TO GARNISH:
black olives
thyme and marjoram
   sprigs (optional)

Mix the dressing ingredients together
in a large bowl, adding salt and
pepper to taste. Stir in the prawns,
cover and chill for 30 minutes.

Cook the pasta until *al dente**.

Drain and cool quickly under cold
running water. Drain thoroughly and
add to the prawns. Carefully stir in
the avocados and herbs.

Transfer the salad to a serving dish
and garnish with black olives, and
thyme and marjoram if liked. Serve
immediately.

Serves 4 to 8

FENNEL AND PASTA SALAD

*500 g (1 lb) dried pasta
   shells or bows*
3 large fennel bulbs, sliced
*2-3 red dessert apples,
   cored and sliced*
juice of 1 lemon
4 spring onions
4 tomatoes
*2 tablespoons sesame
   seeds, toasted*
*50 g (2 oz) salted cashew
   nuts*
DRESSING:
6 tablespoons olive oil
3 tablespoons lemon juice
*1 teaspoon each French
   mustard and honey*
*1 tablespoon each chopped
   parsley and basil*

Cook the pasta until *al dente**. Drain
and cool quickly under cold running
water. Drain thoroughly and place in
a large bowl.

Toss the fennel and apples in the
lemon juice, then add to the pasta.
Chop the spring onions and skin,
seed and chop the tomatoes. Add to
the pasta.

Mix the dressing ingredients
together and pour over the salad.
Transfer to a serving bowl. Sprinkle
with the sesame seeds and cashew
nuts and garnish with fennel leaves, if
liked. Serve immediately.
Serves 4 to 6

PASTA COLESLAW

500 g (1 lb) dried pasta
  twists or shells
1/4-1/2 small red cabbage,
  shredded
1 onion, sliced
1/4 cucumber, diced
2 celery sticks, chopped
2 green dessert apples,
  cored and sliced
juice of 1 lemon
1 bunch of watercress
oil for shallow-frying
4 cloves garlic
2 slices stale bread, cubed

DRESSING:
150 g (5 oz) natural
  yogurt
1-2 cloves garlic, crushed
2 tablespoons each
  chopped parsley and
  chives
pinch of cayenne pepper

Cook the pasta until *al dente**. Drain and cool quickly under cold running water. Drain thoroughly and place in a large bowl. Stir in the cabbage, onion, cucumber and celery.

Toss the apple slices in the lemon juice and add to the bowl with the watercress.

Mix the dressing ingredients together and fold into the salad. Transfer to a serving dish.

Heat the oil in a pan, add the garlic cloves and fry until brown; discard. Add the bread cubes and fry until golden. Drain on kitchen paper and sprinkle over the salad. Serve immediately.

Serves 4 to 8

WINTER SALAD

500 g (1 lb) dried
   tagliatelle verdi
4 celery sticks
1 red pepper
4 red dessert apples
juice of 1 lemon
1/4-1/2 green or white
   cabbage, shredded
125 g (4 oz) black olives
25 g (1 oz) gherkins,
   sliced
25 g (1 oz) sunflower
   seeds, toasted
   (optional)
DRESSING:
4-6 tablespoons
   mayonnaise
2 tablespoons French
   mustard
1 teaspoon lemon juice
1 clove garlic, crushed
2 tablespoons each
   chopped parsley and
   chives
1-2 tablespoons capers,
   drained

Cook the tagliatelle until al dente*.
Drain and cool quickly under cold
running water. Drain thoroughly and
place in a large bowl.

Slice the celery and core, seed and
slice the red pepper. Add to the
tagliatelle.

Core and slice the apples and toss in
the lemon juice. Add to the salad with
the cabbage.

Mix the dressing ingredients
together and carefully mix into the
salad with the olives and gherkins.

Transfer to a serving dish and
sprinkle with the sunflower seeds, if
using. Serve immediately.
Serves 4 to 8

GREEN SALAD WITH NOODLES

150 ml (¼ pint) oil
500 g (1 lb) fresh egg
   noodles
125 g (4 oz) streaky
   bacon, derinded
½ head of curly endive
1 cos lettuce
250 g (8 oz) spinach
1 bunch of watercress
1 bunch of spring onions,
   sliced
2 avocado pears
1 hard-boiled egg
DRESSING:
6 tablespoons olive oil
3 tablespoons lemon juice
1-2 cloves garlic, crushed
½ teaspoon tarragon or
   herb mustard
1 teaspoon honey
1 tablespoon each chopped
   marjoram, parsley and
   thyme

Heat the oil in a wok or large frying pan, add the noodles in batches and fry until golden. Drain on kitchen paper and set aside.

Fry the bacon in its own fat until crisp. Crumble and set aside.

Tear the endive, lettuce and spinach leaves into pieces and place in a deep serving bowl with the watercress and spring onions. Slice the avocados and add to the bowl with the noodles.

Mix the dressing ingredients together, pour over the salad and toss well.

Chop the egg white and sieve the yolk and sprinkle over the salad with the bacon. Serve immediately.
Serves 4 to 6

CHICORY, ORANGE AND PASTA SALAD

500 g (1 lb) fresh
   tagliatelle
4 heads of chicory, sliced
6 large oranges, segmented
2 tablespoons chopped
   tarragon
4 tablespoons snipped
   chives
DRESSING:
6 tablespoons olive oil
2 tablespoons each orange
   and lemon juice
1/2 teaspoon coarse-grain
   mustard
1 teaspoon each honey,
   mixed herbs and finely
   grated orange rind

Cut the tagliatelle into shorter lengths and cook until *al dente**. Drain and cool quickly under cold running water. Drain thoroughly and place in a large bowl.

Mix the dressing ingredients together and pour over the pasta.

Stir in the chicory, orange segments and herbs. Transfer to a serving dish and serve immediately.

Serves 4 to 6

PASTA AND BROAD BEAN SALAD

500 g (1 lb) shelled broad
   beans
salt
500 g (1 lb) dried pasta
   shells or twists
175 g (6 oz) salami, diced
DRESSING:
6 tablespoons mayonnaise
2 eggs, hard-boiled and
   diced
2 tablespoons lime juice
2 teaspoons finely grated
   lime rind
4 tablespoons snipped
   chives
2 tablespoons chopped
   lemon thyme
TO GARNISH:
lemon thyme sprig

Cook the broad beans in boiling salted water for 5 minutes. Drain and set aside.

Cook the pasta until *al dente**. Drain and cool quickly under cold running water. Drain thoroughly and place in a large bowl. Stir in the beans and salami.

Mix the dressing ingredients together and fold into the pasta and beans. Spoon the salad into a serving bowl and garnish with a sprig of lemon thyme.

Serves 4 to 6

NOTE: If you are unable to obtain a lime, use lemon juice and rind instead, but use only 1 tablespoon lemon juice.

KOREAN NOODLES WITH NUTS

125 g (4 oz) mangetouts
2 tablespoons oil
1 onion, sliced
1-2 cloves garlic, sliced
1-2 teaspoons each ground
*   coriander and cumin*
2 dried red chillies
300 g (10 oz) dried
*   vermicelli*
4 spring onions
125 g (4 oz) mushrooms
1 tablespoon chopped
*   coriander*
salt and pepper
50 g (2 oz) pinenuts
50 g (2 oz) flaked
*   almonds, browned*
DRESSING:
4 tablespoons olive oil
2 teaspoons soy sauce
1-2 tablespoons lime juice
1 teaspoon honey

Cook the mangetouts in boiling water
for 1 minute, drain and set aside.

Heat the oil in a pan, add the onion
and cook until golden. Add the
garlic, coriander and cumin, then
crumble in the chillies. Fry over a low
heat for 2 minutes, stirring
constantly. Remove from the heat
and set aside.

Cook the vermicelli until *al dente**.
Drain and cool quickly under cold
running water. Drain thoroughly and
place in a large bowl. Add the cooked
spices and mix well.

Chop the spring onions and slice
the mushrooms. Add to the
vermicelli with the mangetouts and
coriander, and season to taste.

Mix the dressing ingredients
together, pour over the salad and mix
well. Transfer to a serving dish and
sprinkle with the nuts. Garnish with
lime slices and coriander, if liked.
Serves 4 to 6

TAGLIATELLE SALAD

500 g (1 lb) fresh
  wholewheat tagliatelle
2 × 425 g (15 oz) cans
  red kidney beans
2 × 198 g (7 oz) cans
  tuna fish
4 young courgettes
50 g (2 oz) mushrooms
2 small leeks
1 tablespoon green
  peppercorns
DRESSING:
4 tablespoons mayonnaise
2 tablespoons each
  chopped parsley and
  chives
2 teaspoons lemon juice
1 teaspoon finely grated
  lemon rind
cayenne pepper
salt
TO GARNISH:
mint sprigs (optional)
lemon slices

Cook the tagliatelle until *al dente**.
Drain and cool quickly under cold
running water. Drain thoroughly and
place in a large bowl.

Rinse and drain the kidney beans
under cold running water. Drain and
flake the tuna. Thinly slice the
courgettes and mushrooms; chop the
spring onions. Add to the pasta with
the peppercorns.

Mix the dressing ingredients
together, seasoning with cayenne
pepper and salt to taste. Fold into the
salad and transfer to a large serving
bowl.

Garnish with mint sprigs if using,
and lemon slices. Serve immediately.
Serves 4 to 6

PIZZA & PASTA PARTIES

A pizza or pasta party can be a great way to entertain. They are informal and simple to prepare, once you've mastered the basic doughs. These four menus each form a good basis for a party, but do give them your own personal touch by adding favourite ingredients to sauces and toppings.

If you wish to serve a starter, offer an hors d'oeuvre tray. Include a selection of meats and fish – such as salami, garlic sausage, Parma or smoked ham, tongue, sardines, anchovies and tuna fish – with vegetables like artichokes, onion rings, cauliflower florets, mushrooms, celery and peppers, as well as hard-boiled eggs, olives, melon and tomatoes. Arrange them in groups with suitable dressings and attractive garnishes.

If you wish to serve a simple dessert, a fruit salad is always popular. Serve the one on page 91, or make up your own.

Pizza Party for 10
Fennel and Orange Salad
Potato and Dill Salad
Party Pizza
Summer Pudding

Pizza Party for 20
Italian Rice Salad
Mangetout Salad
Chilli Seafood Pizza
Blackcurrant Ice Cream
Lemon Tart

Pasta Party for 15
Greek Salad
Lasagne Verdi al Forno
Italian Fruit Salad

Pasta Party for 20
Broad Bean and Fennel Salad
Creamed Chicken with Noodles
Chocolate and Orange Mousse
Hazelnut and Raspberry Torte

GREEK SALAD

1 kg (2 lb) tomatoes
2 each red and yellow
    peppers, cored
1½ cucumbers, diced
3 onions, sliced
250 g (8 oz) black olives
350 g (12 oz) Feta
    cheese, diced
2 tablespoons chopped
    parsley
DRESSING:
3 × 150 g (5 oz) cartons
    natural yogurt
2 teaspoons Dijon
    mustard
5 tablespoons lemon juice
2 tablespoons finely grated
    lemon rind
3 cloves garlic, crushed
small bunch chopped mint
salt and pepper

First make the dressing: put the yogurt, mustard, lemon juice and rind into a bowl and mix well. Stir in the garlic, mint, and salt and pepper to taste.

Thinly slice the tomatoes and peppers and arrange on a serving plate with the remaining salad ingredients. Spoon over the dressing and toss lightly to serve.

Serves 15

BROAD BEAN AND FENNEL SALAD

1.5 kg (3-3½ lb) shelled
  broad beans
salt and pepper
6 spring onions, chopped
4 heads of fennel, chopped
juice of 2 lemons
50 g (2 oz) flaked
  almonds, toasted
DRESSING:
2-3 cloves garlic, crushed
pinch of cayenne pepper
3 × 150 g (5.2 oz)
  cartons natural yogurt
4 tablespoons chopped
  mint
grated rind of 2 limes

Cook the beans in boiling salted
water for 5 minutes, until just tender.
Drain and cool under cold running
water. Drain thoroughly and place in
a large bowl. Add the spring onions.
Toss the fennel in the lemon juice and
add both to the beans.

Mix the dressing ingredients
together, adding salt and pepper to
taste, spoon over the salad and toss
well.

Pile into a serving dish, sprinkle
with the almonds and garnish with
mint and fennel leaves if liked.
Serves 20

POTATO AND DILL SALAD

1 kg (2 lb) new potatoes
salt and pepper
6 spring onions
7 tablespoons mayonnaise
good pinch of cayenne
    pepper
1 bunch of dill, roughly
    chopped
2 tablespoons sunflower
    seeds, toasted
dill sprigs to garnish

Cook the potatoes in boiling salted water for 15 minutes, until tender. Drain and cool, then slice them into a bowl.

Chop the spring onions into 2.5 cm (1 inch) pieces and add to the bowl with the mayonnaise and cayenne. Season with salt and pepper to taste. Stir in the dill.

Transfer to a serving dish and sprinkle with the sunflower seeds. Garnish with dill to serve.

Serves 10

ITALIAN RICE SALAD

1 chicken carcass
1 bouquet garni
1 large onion
750 g (1½ lb) Italian
    patna rice
150 ml (¼ pint) dry
    white wine
salt and pepper
2 each red, green and
    yellow peppers, cored,
    seeded and chopped
250 g (8 oz) tomatoes,
    seeded and chopped
250 g (8 oz) Italian
    salami, diced
8 basil and 8 oregano
    sprigs, chopped
125 g (4 oz) cashew nuts
DRESSING:
2 teaspoons Dijon
    mustard
6 tablespoons red wine
    vinegar
12 tablespoons olive oil
4 cloves garlic, crushed
3 teaspoons clear honey

Put the chicken carcass in a large pan of cold water with the bouquet garni and onion. Bring to the boil, cover and simmer for 1 to 1½ hours. Strain, reserving the stock. Remove any meat from the bones, chop and set aside.

Place the rice, reserved stock, wine, and salt to taste in a large pan and cook for 12 to 15 minutes, until tender. Drain off any remaining liquid and cool.

Place the rice in a large bowl and stir in the chopped chicken meat.

Mix the dressing ingredients together, seasoning with salt and pepper to taste. Pour over the rice and mix well.

Fold in the remaining ingredients and transfer to a serving dish.

Serves 20

MANGETOUT SALAD

250 g (8 oz) streaky
    bacon, derinded
1 kg (2 lb) mangetouts
salt and pepper
2 tablespoons each
    chopped thyme and
    parsley
DRESSING:
2 teaspoons peppercorn
    mustard
4 cloves garlic, crushed
2 teaspoons clear honey
4 tablespoons lime juice
8 tablespoons olive oil
3 tablespoons chopped
    parsley
2 tablespoons chopped
    thyme

Grill the bacon until crisp. Leave to cool, then crumble or chop and set aside.

Mix all the dressing ingredients together, seasoning with salt and pepper to taste.

Blanch the mangetouts in boiling salted water for 2 minutes. Drain, cool under cold running water and drain thoroughly.

Toss the mangetouts in the dressing, then mix in the bacon and chopped herbs. Transfer to a serving dish and garnish with lime slices and parsley if liked.
Serves 20

PARTY PIZZA

1½ quantity pizza dough*
1½ quantity Tomato
    Sauce (see American
    Hot Pizza, page 30)
125 g (4 oz) button
    mushrooms, sliced
8 canned artichoke hearts,
    sliced
6 tomatoes, sliced
6 oregano sprigs
1 × 198 g (7 oz) can tuna
    fish, drained
2 tablespoons capers
2 × 50 g (1¾ oz) cans
    anchovies, drained
50 g (2 oz) green olives,
    chopped
125 g (4 oz) salami
50 g (2 oz) Mozzarella
    cheese, diced
125 g (4 oz) ham
50 g (2 oz) sweetcorn
2 teaspoons dried mixed
    herbs
2 tablespoons olive oil
75 g (3 oz) matured
    Cheddar cheese, grated

Roll out the dough to fit a large baking sheet, measuring 25 × 30 cm (10 × 12 inches); turn during rolling to prevent shrinking.

Place on a large piece of floured cardboard. Using fingertips, push the dough out from the centre to make the edges twice as thick as the rest.

Spread with the tomato sauce. Using a palette knife, lightly divide the dough into 6 sections.

Arrange the mushrooms and artichokes in one section; the tomatoes and oregano in another; the flaked tuna and capers in the third; the mashed anchovies and olives in the fourth; the sliced salami and Mozzarella cheese in the fifth; and the sliced ham and sweetcorn in the last section.

Sprinkle the whole pizza with the mixed herbs, oil and grated cheese.

Slide the pizza onto the hot baking sheet* and bake in a preheated hot oven, 230°C (450°F), Gas Mark 8, for 15 to 20 minutes. Cut into slices and serve immediately.
Serves 10

CHILLI SEAFOOD PIZZA

3 × quantity pizza
    dough*

3 × quantity Tomato
    Sauce (see American
    Hot Pizza, page 30)

2 tablespoons dried
    oregano

8 green chilli peppers,
    seeded and thinly sliced

3 × 198 g (7 oz) cans
    tuna fish, drained and
    flaked

300 g (10 oz) peeled
    prawns

350 g (12 oz) Bel Paese
    cheese, grated

2 × 50 g (1¾ oz) cans
    anchovies, drained

125 g (4 oz) stuffed
    olives, halved

Roll out the dough to fit 3 large baking sheets, measuring 25 × 30 cm (10 × 12 inches). Turn the dough during rolling to prevent shrinking.

Place on 2 or 3 large pieces of floured cardboard. Using the fingertips, push the dough from the centre outwards to make the edges twice as thick as the rest.

Spread with the tomato sauce and sprinkle with the oregano. Spoon over the chillies, tuna and prawns, and sprinkle with the cheese. Arrange the anchovies in a lattice over the top and decorate with the olives.

Slide the pizza onto the hot baking sheets* and bake in a preheated hot oven, 230°C (450°F), Gas Mark 8, for 15 to 20 minutes. Serve immediately.
Serves 20

LASAGNE VERDI AL FORNO

8 tablespoons olive oil
3 onions, chopped
6 cloves garlic, crushed
4 celery sticks, chopped
1 kg (2 lb) minced beef
250 g (8 oz) chicken
    livers, chopped
salt and pepper
900 ml (1½ pints) dry
    white wine
3 × 397 g (14 oz) cans
    tomatoes
1 teaspoon grated nutmeg
2 teaspoons dried mixed
    herbs
12 sheets dried lasagne
    verdi
300 ml (½ pint)
    Béchamel sauce (see
    Baked Rigatoni, page
    53)
125 g (4 oz) Parmesan
    cheese, grated
25 g (1 oz) matured
    Cheddar cheese, grated
2 tablespoons dried
    breadcrumbs

Heat the oil in a large pan, add the onions and 4 cloves garlic and cook for 10 minutes, until pale golden. Stir in the celery and cook for 2 minutes.

Increase the heat and add the minced beef. Cook rapidly until lightly browned. Add the chicken livers, and season liberally with salt and pepper.

Pour over the wine, add the tomatoes with their juice, nutmeg and herbs. Bring to the boil, cover and simmer very gently for 2½ to 3 hours, stirring occasionally; if the mixture becomes too thick, add a little more wine. Stir in the remaining garlic and check the seasoning.

Spoon enough sauce into a very large ovenproof dish or roasting pan to cover the base. Arrange some lasagne over this. Repeat the layers until all the sauce and lasagne are used, finishing with lasagne.

Spoon over the Béchamel sauce and sprinkle with the cheeses and breadcrumbs.

Bake in a preheated moderately hot oven, 200°C (400°F), Gas Mark 6, for 45 to 50 minutes, until golden. Serve immediately.
Serves 15

CREAMED CHICKEN WITH NOODLES

2 × 2.25 kg (5 lb) oven-
  ready chickens
3 large onions, halved
1 bottle dry white wine
1 large bouquet garni
salt and pepper
125 g (4 oz) butter
8 shallots, chopped
3-4 cloves garlic, crushed
1 kg (2 lb) tomatoes,
  skinned, seeded and
  chopped
2 tablespoons each
  chopped basil and
  parsley
3 tablespoons chopped
  thyme
2 × 284 ml (½ pint)
  cartons double cream
2 kg (4½ lb) fresh
  tagliatelle
125 g (4 oz) butter
fresh herbs to garnish

Place the chickens in a large roasting pan. Add the onions, wine, bouquet garni, and salt and pepper to taste. Cover with foil and cook in a preheated moderate oven, 180°C (350°F), Gas Mark 4, for 2½ hours, until very tender; cool.

Remove the flesh from the chickens and cut into small pieces. Remove the fat from the top of the liquid and strain the stock.

Melt the butter in a large pan, add the shallots and garlic and cook gently for 10 minutes. Add the tomatoes and herbs, and season with salt and pepper. Stir in the strained stock.

Bring to the boil, cover and simmer for 40 minutes. Remove lid and cook rapidly until thickened. Stir in the cream and chicken; set aside.

Cook the tagliatelle in 2 large pans until *al dente**. Drain and return to the pans. Divide the butter between the pans and toss well.

Heat the sauce, without boiling, pour over the pasta and toss well.

Transfer to a warmed serving dish and garnish with herbs. Serve with grated Parmesan cheese.

Serves 20

BLACKCURRANT ICE CREAM

1.5 kg (3 lb) fresh or
  frozen blackcurrants
550 g (18 oz) caster sugar
900 ml (1½ pints) water
grated rind and juice of
  1 lemon
1.25 litres (2¼ pints)
  double cream, lightly
  whipped

Place the blackcurrants in a large pan, with the sugar, water, lemon rind and juice. Bring to the boil, cover and simmer for 12 to 15 minutes, until the fruit is soft.

Leave to cool, then place the fruit and syrup in a food processor or an electric blender and work until smooth. Rub through a nylon sieve to remove pips. Fold the fruit purée into the cream.

Spoon the mixture into a rigid freezerproof container and freeze until firm. Remove from the freezer and whisk well. Refreeze for 2 hours, then whisk again. Return the ice cream to the container, cover, seal and freeze until firm.

Transfer to the refrigerator 30 minutes before serving to soften. Spoon into chilled dishes to serve.
Serves 12 to 16

SUMMER PUDDING

1 kg (2 lb) mixed summer
  fruits, e.g.
  blackcurrants,
  raspberries, redcurrants
175-250 g (6-8 oz) sugar
12 trifle sponge cakes

Put the fruits in a large saucepan, cover and bring slowly to the boil. Simmer for 7 to 10 minutes. Remove from the heat, stir in the sugar to taste and leave to cool.

Slice the sponge cakes in half lengthways and use to line the base and sides of a 1.5 litre (2½ pint) pudding basin. Spoon in three quarters of the stewed fruit and top with the remaining sponge cakes. Spoon over a little more fruit. Cover with a saucer or plate, gently pushing down. Leave in the refrigerator overnight.

Remove the plate, run a palette knife around the edge of the pudding and turn out onto a deep serving plate. Spoon over the remaining fruit and serve with whipped cream.
Serves 10

LEMON TART

PASTRY:

175 g (6 oz) plain flour

2 tablespoons caster sugar

*125 g (4 oz) cold butter,
cut into small pieces*

1 egg yolk

FILLING:

175 g (6 oz) sugar

*150 ml (¼ pint) fresh
lemon juice*

*120 ml (4 fl oz) orange
juice*

grated zest of 3 lemons

4 eggs

50 g (2 oz) butter

*4 tablespoons double
cream*

TO FINISH:

*2 lemons, cut into
segments*

icing sugar, sifted

Sift the flour onto a pastry board and stir in the sugar. Make a hollow in the centre and add the butter and egg yolk. Using the fingertips, lightly bring the flour mixture into the centre over the butter and egg to combine the ingredients. Knead lightly and form into a ball. Dust with flour, cover with clingfilm and chill for 1 hour.

Roll out the dough and use to line a 25 cm (10 inch) flan tin with removable base. Prick with a fork and chill for 1 hour. Line the pastry case with greaseproof paper and dried beans and bake in a preheated moderately hot oven, 200°C (400°F), Gas Mark 6, for 10 to 15 minutes, until lightly browned. Remove the greaseproof paper and baking beans.

Place the sugar, lemon and orange juice, zest and eggs in a bowl and beat together. Melt the butter in a pan, stir in the cream, add the egg mixture and cook over a low heat, stirring, until thickened; take care not to scramble the eggs and do not boil. Remove from the heat, transfer to a bowl and cover the surface with dampened greaseproof paper. Cover the bowl with clingfilm and leave to cool.

Spoon the custard into the pastry case and bake in a preheated moderately hot oven, 190°C (375°F), Gas Mark 5, for 20 minutes.

Arrange the lemon segments on top and sprinkle liberally with icing sugar. Place under a preheated hot grill for 1 minute until golden brown. Serve warm or cold with cream.

Serves 10 to 12

NOTE: If you think most of your guests will want a portion of each dessert make two of these tarts.

ITALIAN FRUIT SALAD

600 ml (1 pint) orange
  juice
grated rind of 2 lemons
6 tablespoons lemon juice
125 g (4 oz) black
  cherries
1/2 Galia melon
3 bananas
4 nectarines
1 mango
3 peaches
125 g (4 oz) apricots
4 green dessert apples
2 pears
125 g (4 oz) white
  seedless grapes
25-50 (1-2 oz) caster
  sugar
10 tablespoons
  Maraschino liqueur

Put the orange juice, lemon rind and juice in a large bowl.

Prepare the fruit, adding to the bowl as you do so: stone the cherries, scoop the melon into small balls using a melon baller; slice the bananas; stone and slice the nectarines, mango, peaches and apricots; core and slice the apples and pears. Add the grapes and stir well.

Sprinkle over the sugar to taste and the Maraschino and stir well. Cover and chill for 1 hour.

Serve with cream and crisp biscuits.
Serves 15

CHOCOLATE AND ORANGE MOUSSE

350 g (12 oz) plain
  chocolate
40 g (1½ oz) butter
6 eggs, separated
grated rind and juice of
  2 oranges
2 tablespoons brandy
TO DECORATE:
142 ml (5 fl oz) double
  cream, whipped
2 chocolate flakes, broken
  into pieces

Break the chocolate into a heatproof
bowl over a pan of hot water. Stir
occasionally until melted, then stir in
the butter and blend well. Add the
egg yolks and mix well. Remove
from the heat. Stir in the orange rind
and juice and the brandy.

Whisk the egg whites until very
stiff and fold into the chocolate
mixture. Transfer to a serving dish
and chill for 3 hours.

Decorate with whipped cream and
chocolate flake to serve.
Serves 10 to 12

HAZELNUT AND RASPBERRY TORTE

250 g (8 oz) hazelnuts
150 g (5 oz) plain flour
salt
125 g (4 oz) icing sugar,
  sifted
125 g (4 oz) unsalted
  butter, softened
1 egg yolk
FILLING:
284 ml (10 fl oz)
  whipping cream,
  whipped
75 g (3 oz) cranberry
  sauce
250 g (8 oz) fresh
  raspberries
TO DECORATE:
120 ml (4 fl oz) double
  cream, whipped
whole raspberries
hazelnuts, toasted

Place the hazelnuts under a hot grill for a few minutes to brown. Remove the skins and grind coarsely.

Sift the flour and a pinch of salt on to a board. Make a well in the centre, put in the hazelnuts, icing sugar, butter and egg yolk. Work the flour into the centre, using the fingertips, and mix to a smooth paste. Cover and chill for 1 hour.

Divide the dough into 4. Roll out each piece into a 20 cm (8 inch) circle and place on lightly greased baking sheets. Prick each circle with a fork and chill for 1 hour.

Bake in a preheated moderately hot oven, 190°C (375°F), Gas Mark 5, for 8 to 10 minutes, until golden. Cool on wire racks.

Place one round on a serving plate. Mix together the whipped cream and cranberry sauce and use a third to cover the biscuit base. Cover with a third of the raspberries and place another biscuit round on top. Repeat the layers twice more, finishing with a biscuit round.

Spread half the whipped cream in a thin layer over the top of the torte; use the remaining cream to pipe rosettes around the edge. Finish with raspberries and hazelnuts.

Serves 12

NOTE: If you think all of your guests will choose the torte, double the quantities and make two!

INDEX

ACKNOWLEDGMENTS
Photography by Charlie Stebbings
Food prepared by Caroline Ellwood
Photographic stylist: Liz Hipsley